ISBN 978-0-483-54781-0
PIBN 10787944

A HELP

TO

FAMILY WORSHIP,

OR

SHORT FORMS OF

MORNING AND EVENING PRAYERS

FOR FOUR WEEKS.

WITH

PRAYERS FOR SPECIAL OCCASIONS, GRACE AT TABLE,
CHILDREN'S MORNING AND EVENING PRAYERS,
AND MORNING AND EVENING HYMNS.

COMPILED BY

P. ANSTADT, D. D.,

EDITOR TEACHERS' JOURNAL, CHRISTIAN'S GUIDE, AUTHOR OF
BIBLE WINE, COMMUNION ADDRESSES, ILLUSTRATED
CATECHISM, ETC., ETC.

YORK, PA.
P. ANSTADT & SONS,
1894.

PREFACE.

These short Forms of Prayer are intended to be a help in conducting Family Worship. They are not designed to interfere with the free utterance of prayer by the heads of families in their own words. But it is well known that many pious christians are not well qualified to lead in public worship. Some are diffident, or have not had the proper mental training, and have not command of appropriate words to edify in social prayer. It is to such mainly, that this book is to be a help.

We hope also it will be a means of introducing family worship in households, where it would, without this help, perhaps, have never been introduced. Besides this, even the most cultivated christian minds may obtain spiritual edification by the perusal of well prepared forms of prayer, where their exclusive use can be dispensed with in family worship.

In providing these forms, therefore, we venture to express the hope, that none will use them formally, slavishly, or exclusively. They are of necessity *general* in their terms, and cannot set forth special circumstances. Let such be added in his own words, as occasion may arise, by the person who conducts the worship. The various subjects of prayer and praise included here, gives full opportunity for introducing in their proper place and connection such special topics, as well as those petitions of a more general kind, which may from time to time be suggested to the mind.

As a general rule, family prayer should be preceded

by the reading of Scripture.   The singing of a hymn, either
before or after the prayer, will help to promote devotional
feelings, and make the daily family worship interesting and
attractive to the children, as well as older members of the
household.   The passage of Scripture read will often suggest subjects of prayer.   For these it is obviously impossi-
ble to provide a form.   In many cases the very words of
Scripture, just read, may be turned into prayer.   What can
more fitly follow a promise than a prayer for its fulfillment?
When a holy example has been set forth, it seems but right
and natural to follow it.

Let each person ask in silence beforehand for a collected mind, and for the spirit of prayer, " Lord, teach us to
pray!"   Let this be the desire and prayer of each in kneeling before God.   Nor let it ever be forgotten, that we have
a great High Priest, through whom alone we have access
to God, and that ".the Spirit also helpeth our infirmities."

We lay no claim to originality in these Forms of
Prayer.   Some parts of them are of our own composing,
but the most of them were arranged, rewritten, and compiled from other works.

YORK, 1894.   P. ANSTADT.

AFTER MORNING OR EVENING PRAYER.

OUR Father, who art in heaven, Hallowed be Thy name. Thy kingdom come. Thy will be done on earth, as it is in heaven. Give us this day (*or*, day by day) our daily bread. And forgive us our trespasses, as we forgive them that trespass against us. And lead us not into temptation; but deliver us from evil. For Thine is the kingdom, the power, and the glory, for ever and ever. Amen.

SCRIPTURAL FORMS OF BLESSING.

THE grace of our Lord Jesus Christ, and the love of God, and the fellowship of the Holy Ghost, be with us all evermore. Amen.

THE peace of God, which passeth all understanding, keep our hearts and minds in the knowledge and love of God, and of His Son Jesus Christ our Lord: and the blessing of God Almighty, the Father, the Son, and the Holy Ghost, be amongst us, and remain with us always. Amen.

THE Lord bless us, and keep us; the Lord make his face to shine upon us, and be gracious unto us. The Lord lift up his countenance upon us, and give us peace, both now and evermore. Amen.

THE God of peace, that brought again from the dead our Lord Jesus, that great Shepherd of the sheep, through the blood of the everlasting covenant, make us perfect in every good work to do his will, working in us that which is well pleasing in his sight, through Jesus Christ, to whom be glory, forever and ever. Amen.

FAMILY PRAYERS.

SUNDAY MORNING.

DOUBTLESS thou art our Father.—Isa. lxiii. 16.
One God and Father of all, who is above all, and through all, and in you all.—Eph. iv. 6.

Almighty God, our heavenly Father, we thank thee for the light of this new Sabbath morning, which we have been permitted to see in so much favor and mercy. And now, as the natural sun has arisen and dispelled the darkness and spread the beautiful light of day over the earth, so let the light of thy countenance shine upon us. O, do thou enlighten us with wisdom from on high. May this day our faith be strengthened, may our hopes be brightened, may our hearts be warmed with love to God and man, may all our christian graces be renewed and strengthened

We confess our unworthiness, our natural depravity and corruption, and our sins and shortcomings in practice. Lord, subdue within us whatever is contrary to thy mind and will. May our hearts become living temples and our lives living sacrifices. May we daily grow in the grace of God and in the knowledge of Christ.

For the sake of *Jesus Christ*, the Son of thy love, have thou mercy upon us miserable offenders. We bring the burden of daily transgression to the Lamb of God, who taketh away the sin of the world. In him receive us graciously and love us freely. By a living faith in him may we be enabled to take up the song of the redeemed and pardoned, " O Lord, we will praise thee ; though thou wast angry with us, thine anger is turned away and thou dost comfort us : Behold, God is our salvation ; we will trust and not be afraid ; for the Lord God is our strength and our song, he also is become our salvation."

Bless us as a family and a household. As we are bound together in earthly ties, do thou unite us also in the better bands of the everlasting covenant. Make us all partakers of the resurrection life of thy people ; so that though death may sooner or later separate us here, we may meet in heaven, where there is no more separation. We commend all who are near and dear to us to thy sovereign care.

We pray for the poor, the afflicted, the bereaved and the dying. O thou comforter of all those that are cast down, do thou heal their sorrows and bind up their wounds.

We pray for those who shall this day minister in thy holy sanctuary. Give them an unction from the Holy Ghost. May every impression of thy word be rendered permanent and saving. May we be in the Spirit on the Lord's day and pitch our tents near the gate of heaven. And when we shall no longer worship thee in temples here on earth, may we be received into that house not made with hands, whose builder and maker is God, eternal in the heavens ; and thou, Father, Son and Holy Ghost shalt have all the praise, now and evermore. Amen.

SUNDAY EVENING.

YOUR reward shall be great, and ye shall be the children of the
Highest: for he is kind unto the unthankful and to the evil.—
Luke vi. 35.

Our Heavenly Father, we desire to close this Holy
Sabbath day, in looking up to thee for a blessing. We thank
thee for all the tokens of thy mercy which we have enjoyed
this day. And now as the night has closed around us let
thy banner over us be love.

We bless and praise thee for thine unspeakable gift, the
Son of thy love, to become our Redeemer. All our hope
of salvation comes from him. We rejoice that Jesus is as
willing as he is able "to save to the uttermost," all who
will come to God through him. Lord, we come, casting
ourselves on the fulness of thy grace, in him. Sanctify us
wholly, in body, soul and spirit. Subdue our wills, and
bring them into entire obedience to thy most holy will.
When called to the performance of any duty or the endur-
ance of any trial, may we say from our hearts, "Lord, here
am I. Thy will be done." O that thy love may be enthroned as the ruling passion of our souls, and thy glory
the end of our being. Fulfill in our experience thine own
gracious promise: "I will dwell in them, and walk with
them, and I will be their God, and they shall be my people."

We entreat thee graciously to forgive the many sins that
have mingled in our efforts to serve thee. If we were to be
judged even by our holiest services, we should stand condemned. Look not on us as we are in ourselves, but look
on the face of thine Anointed, thy Son Jesus Christ, who
has made atonement for all our sins. We would cleave to
him as our only Savior. Enable us to manifest the reality
of our faith, by doing good works as the fruit of that living

faith, and by a holy life and conversation. May thy love reign supreme within us. May we show by our pure lives and christian walk, that we have imbibed the spirit of Christ. Take these erring hearts, sanctify and seal them for thyself; make them thine; thine only; and thine wholly; and thine forever. Clothe us with the spotless righteousness of Christ. Let not the things of this world exclude from our minds and hearts the blessings of the world to come. May it be our great aim to advance in the divine life. May we ever hear thy voice saying, " Arise and depart ye, for this is not your rest ! " May our habitual response be—" We desire a better country, that is an heavenly."

We pray for a world lying in wickedness. How long, O how long, shall the wicked triumph ! Save thy people and bless thine inheritance ; glorify thyself in the salvation of sinners. May the hands of thy ministering servants be made strong by the arm of the Almighty God of hosts.

Do thou follow with thy rich blessing all the services of the sanctuary this day. May thy word be quick and powerful upon the hearts and consciences of the hearers. May the impressions made, not die away, but remain deep and lasting.

We commit ourselves to thy care this night. Do thou watch over us during the unconscious hours of sleep. May 'we awake in the morning in thy favor ; so that every new day, being spent to thy glory, may find us better fitted for entering on the joys of thine everlasting kingdom ; through Jesus Christ, our Savior. Amen.

MONDAY MORNING.

A ND I looked, and, lo, a Lamb stood on the mount Sion, and with
him an hundred forty and four thousand, having his Father's
name written in their foreheads.—Rev. xiv. 1.

O Lord, thou art the King of kings and Lord of lords.
Angels and archangels adore thee, seraphim and cherubim
veil their faces in thy presence, and cry out, holy, holy, holy
is the Lord of Hosts, heaven and earth are full of his glory.
We who are also the creatures of thy hand and the pension-
ers on thy bounty, would unite with saints and angels in
this thrice holy that resounds before thy throne. Thou
hast endowed us with rational minds and immortal souls,
and thou hast sent thy Son into the world to redeem us
from sin and eternal death and make us eternally and unspeakably happy. Blessed be thy name that though thou
art the greatest of all beings, thou dost stoop to hear our
prayers and listen to our wants.

Blessed Savior, thou art waiting to be gracious. All
the mighty load of our guilt we would transfer to thee, our
adorable surety. Thou hast already satisfied the require-
ments of a righteous law. As our kinsman and elder
brother thou art now within the veil; as willing as thou
ever wast to save unto the uttermost.

O God, let it be our constant aim to know what thy
will is; and may we have strength given us to obey it.
May we cheerfully submit to all the dispensations of thy
Providence; whether it be joy or sorrow, prosperity or adversity, health or sickness, life or death, and be enabled
from our hearts to say, "Thy will be done," assured that
thy will is the best for us. Fill our hearts with love to thee,

and enable us to profess, " Lord, thou knowest all things, thou knowest that we love thee."

God of Bethel, dwell in this household; make every member of it a member of the household of faith. Bless all our friends. Those who are absent, Lord, be near them. Those that are in distress, Lord, comfort them. Those who know thee not, Lord, reveal thyself to them. Those who are thy children, do thou increase their devotedness.

Prosper thy cause and kingdom everywhere. Let Satan's kingdom be destroyed—the kingdom of grace advanced—the kingdom of glory hastened.

We come anew, casting ourselves on the infinite fullness of our adorable Redeemer. In him is all our hope. Transform us into his image. May we seek to walk in his footsteps, and to follow his example. May all who see us take knowledge of us that we have been with Jesus and learned of him humility and love.

O Lord, our heavenly Father, we are pilgrims and sojourners here, as all our fathers were. We are wandering through this wilderness world toward the heavenly Canaan, the home which thou hast promised to all who truly love and serve thee. May we make the salvation of our souls, the welfare of our fellowmen and the glory of God our constant aim. May we walk in that straight and narrow path that leads to eternal life, turning neither to the right nor to the left, but press on toward the mark of our high calling, looking to Christ Jesus, the author and finisher of our faith. We ask every blessing in the name of Christ. Amen.

MONDAY EVENING.

WILT thou not from this time cry unto me, My father?—
Jer. iii. 4.

Return, ye backsliding children, and I will heal your backslid-
ings. Behold, we come unto thee; for thou art the Lord our God.—
Jer. iii. 22.

O Lord God Almighty, who hast graciously shielded
us through another day, we desire, ere we retire to rest, to
commit ourselves; soul and body, to thy tender care for the
night. Glory be to our God for all the blessings of the
light; and now, as the curtain of night is again drawn
around us, do thou give thy holy angels charge over us that
no evil may befall us and no danger come near our dwelling. It is thou, Lord, only, who makest us to dwell in
safety.

We acknowledge thee as our daily benefactor and
guardian. Thine is the air we breathe, the food we eat, the
raiment with which we are clothed and the homes in which
we dwell. But far above all these temporal gifts, we bless
thee for Jesus, the Son of thy love. He is our only and all-
sufficient Savior; his is the only name given by which we
can be saved. We would rejoice anew in the assurance,
that his blood cleanseth us from all sin; and that he is able
and willing to save to the uttermost. We rejoice to know
that he is at this moment pleading in behalf of his people;—
the Wonderful Counsellor;—the Prince, who hath power
with God and must at all times prevail.

May we be richly endowed with his spirit, and clothed
in his righteousness. Make us like him, patient and meek,
thankful and forgiving. Take away all pride, vain
glory and hypocricy—all absorbing love of this world.

Set our affections on things above, and enable us to use things temporal, so that we lose not the things eternal.

O Lord God, we thank thee that thou hast established a great kingdom on earth, and hast appointed thine own beloved Son to be the king over it. Help us to come into this kingdom, not merely as nominal members of it, but by sincere repententance of our sins and by a living faith in Jesus Christ. We bless thee, O God, for the promises of pardon and the appointed means of grace; may we be cleansed from our sins by the washing of regeneration, may we be baptized not only with water, but also by the Holy Spirit, who will sanctify our hearts and lead us into the knowledge of all necessary truth and the practice of every christian virtue. And having ourselves become members of Christ's kingdom, we would pray that this kingdom may be everywhere extended in our own land and to the ends of the earth, and thy name be glorified, so that all men may see the salvation of God. May we ever regard Jesus Christ as the only begotten of the Father, full of grace and truth. And since he has condescended to come down from the very bosom of the Father to instruct us in his nature and will, we would most humbly receive thy commands, and earnestly pray that we may so know God as faithfully to serve him now, and at length enjoy him forever.

To thy tender care we commit ourselves this night. In thy keeping we shall be safe. Give thy holy angels charge of us to keep us; may we rest securely under the shadow of thy wings. If it be thy holy will, give us undisturbed repose and refreshing sleep to prepare us for the duties of the coming day, if it is thy good pleasure that we shall see its returning light. We ask all for the sake of Jesus Christ, our Lord. Amen.

TUESDAY MORNING.

HE that spared not his own Son, but deliverod him up for us all, how shall he not with him also freely give us all things?— Rom. viii 32.

We thank thee, O Lord God, for thy guardian care over us during the darkness of the night, for undisturbed repose, for refreshing sleep, and for the returning light of a new day. O Lord, we realize that our days and nights, our weeks and months and years are passing on and bearing their records with them. Help us so to number our days that we may apply our hearts unto wisdom; help us to work and do thy will while it is day, for there is no work or device in the grave, whither we are hastening.

O Lord Jesus, thou didst come into this world to endure the shame and agony of the cross in order to redeem our souls from eternal death and hell. We would confess thee with our lips; we would confess thee in the great congregation of thy church; we would confess thee before the world; we would confess thee in our lives by a holy walk and conversation; we would confess thee in death as our only hope of a life beyond the grave. And O Lord Jesus, thou wilt also confess us before thy Father and our Father, and before the holy angels in the kingdom of heaven. Make us willing, O Christ, to take up our cross and follow thee, through ignomy and shame and even persecution from the world. Help us to persevere in this good warfare even unto the end, and then shall we be able to exclaim with Paul, " I am now ready, I have fought a good fight, I have finished my course, I have kept the faith, and now there is laid up for me a crown of righteousness, which Christ, the righteous Judge shall give me in that day, and not to me only, but to all those who love his appearing."

Bless all in sorrow, heal thou the wounds of their hearts. May they bow in submission to thy will, and say, " It is good for us that we have been afflicted. May those laid on beds of sickness, exercise patience under bodily pain and infirmity ; may useful lives be spared and the dying be prepared for death.

Hasten the promised times of refreshing from the Lord. May Jesus take to himself his great power and reign. Let the day soon come, when he shall have dominion from sea to sea, and from the river unto the ends of the earth, when all kings shall fall down before him, and all nations shall serve him. Hasten the time when wars shall cease in the earth, when nation shall not lift up the sword against nation, when they shall beat their swords into plow shares and their spears into pruning hooks, and men shall learn war no more. Give peace in our time, O God, for there is none other that fighteth successfully for us, but only thou O God. If thou, O God, art for us, then none can be successfully against us.

Bless this family and house-hold ; may we all know the happiness of the shepherds' fold. Take us this day under thy peculiar care. The Lord bless us and keep us— the Lord cause his face to shine on us—the Lord be gracious unto us and give us peace for Jesus sake. Amen.

TUESDAY EVENING.

NOW our Lord Jesus Christ himself, and God, even our Father, which hath loved us, and hath given us everlasting consolation and good hope through grace, comfort your hearts, and establish you in every good word and work.—2 Thess. ii. 16, 17.

O Lord, we draw near to the throne of grace at the close of this day to thank thee for the goodness and mercy that have followed us thus far. But above all we thank thee for thine infinite love in the redemption of the world by the Lord Jesus, for the means of grace and for the hope of glory. We thank thee that thy well-beloved Son has brought in an everlasting righteousness; that he has fulfilled thy law and made it honorable; that he has suffered on Golgotha to atone for our sins; that he has dispelled the darkness of the valley of death and opened the gates of heaven to all believers.

O Lord Jesus, we adore thee, we praise thee, we magnify thy name; for thou hast redeemed us with thine own most precious blood, and made us kings and priests unto God. How shall we sufficiently praise thee for all thy goodness to us, and how can we ever recompense thee for all thy loving kindness! Words can not express and our hearts cannot conceive the debt of gratitude which we owe to thee. All that we can do in return, is to give ourselves to thee, a living sacrifice. Here, Lord, we give ourselves to thee, soul and body, all that we have and are. O do thou accept us graciously and love us freely. Whom have we in heaven but thee, and there is none on earth that we desire beside thee. O Lord, sanctify us, soul and body, and make us pure in heart, that we may finally obtain the blessing which Jesus promised, when he said, Blessed are the pure in heart, for they shall see God.

Nothing else, but the merits of our blessed Redeemer can save us. We come to thee, O Christ, for salvation. Our souls would magnify the Lord, our spirits would rejoice in God our Savior; for he that is mighty hath done great things for us, and holy is his name.

And while we look by faith to his atonement, as the only ground of our justification, we would look to the Holy Spirit to work in us all the good pleasure of his goodness. May he mould us after the Savior's image, and conform us to his will. Lord, give us a supreme love to thee and fervent charity to all men; may we seek to live, as we would wish we had been living, when we come to die.

Have mercy on the afflicted in body, soul or estate. Let them submit to thy will and rest in thy love. Let them rejoice in him who is their brother in the flesh, and sympathizes with them in all their trials; and if they see not the bright light in the cloud, may they trust thine own promise. " At the evening time it shall be light."

Promote thy cause and kingdom in the world. Pour out upon the ministers, and missionaries and churches the healthful Spirit of thy grace. May the time soon come when all the ends of the earth shall see the salvation of God.

Bless our own family and household, those nearest and dearest to us. May the peace of God keep their hearts. Number them with thy saints in glory everlasting. Be with us through this night. May our bodies be refreshed with sleep; and may we awake to the duties of a new day, with our minds staid on thee. And unto thy great name, Father, Son and Holy Spirit, we ascribe blessing, and honor, and glory, and praise, now and forever. Amen.

WEDNESDAY MORNING.

HOW shall I put thee among the children, and give thee a pleasant
land, a goodly heritage of the hosts of nations? and I said,
Thou shalt call me, My Father; and shall not turn away from me.—
Jere. iii. 19.

O Christ, thou light of the world, how can we sufficiently thank and adore thee for thine infinite love. Thou
didst forsake thy throne of glory in heaven, the adoration
of holy angels, and didst come down into this world of sin
and sorrow to assume our nature, and become our brother
in the flesh. Thou didst bring the light of heaven to earth
and reveal it unto men. Oh let the sun of righteousness
also arise upon us in our darkness and illuminate our minds
with the light from heaven. Angels and seraphim might
well be amazed at the deep abasements of our adorable Redeemer, who, though King of kings and Lord of lords, was
born in a stable and cradled in a manger. Yet, O blessed
Jesus, how much more venerable was that stable and manger when graced by thy sacred presence, than the most
magnificent palace or shining throne! How ill does it become poor sinners to be proud of the vain pomp and grand-
eur of this world.

Lord, be thou our Covenant God. Thy presence hal-
lows all joy, sweetens all sorrow, and takes the sting from
every thorn and every cross. If we have thy favor and
blessing we are independent of any other. Heart and flesh
faileth, but thou art the strength of our heart and our portion forever.

We pray for the afflicted. Be a father to the fatherless, a husband to the widow, the orphan's stay, and the
stranger's shield. Let every heavy laden one know that it
is *thy* gracious hand that appoints every burden. Give us

all grace to be resigned to thy will. May this be the breathing of our hearts, " Father, glorify thy name."

Hasten, Lord, thy kingdom. Bring in thine ancient people with the fulness of the Gentile nations. Prosper the labors of thy missionary servants ; may the Lord stand by them and strengthen them. May they not be afraid of evil tidings ; may their hearts be fixed, trusting in the Lord.

May each of us feel, that in our several spheres we have some work to perform for thee. Let the solemn word of warning be ever sounding in our ears, " The night cometh wherein none of us can work." O, may we be diligent, that we may at last be found of him in peace, without spot and blameless.

Bless our household and friends : may they all be thy friends and may we all have a family resemblance to the great head of the church, Jesus Christ, our Elder Brother. Our moments are gliding swiftly by; forbid that any among us should be seeking oil, like the foolish virgins, when the lamp of life is going out. Let us be always living with eternity in view ; let us die daily to sin, and live daily to God, that when the hour of our departure arrives, it may be to all of us the birthday of a new life in glory everlasting. We ask all these blessings for ourselves and for others in the name and for the sake of our adorable Lord and Savior, who is within the veil interceding for us and who ever liveth and reigneth, world without end. Amen.

WEDNESDAY EVENING.

IF ye endure chastening, God dealeth with you as with sons; for what son is he whom the father chasteneth not?—Heb. xii. 7.

O Lord Jesus, teach us to pray, as thou didst also teach thy disciples to pray. And when we pray with our lips may we also pray in our hearts. Thou, O God, art a Spirit, and they who would worship thee aright must worship thee in spirit and in truth. We pray for the coming of thy kingdom, not only in the world, but also in our own hearts, that we may do thy will on earth as the angels do thy will in heaven. Do thou supply all our daily wants, both spiritual and temporal. Forgive our sins for Christ's sake, and help us also to forgive our enemies from our hearts, as we hope to be forgiven by thee. Lead us evermore by thy Holy Spirit in the right way, that straight and narrow way that leads to life, and help us to shun the broad and downward way that leads to destruction. May we never permit ourselves to be led along by the multitudes to do evil, but keep close to thee, our God and Savior, and by thy side and in thy hand we shall ever be safe. For thine is the kingdom and the power and the glory forever and ever.

O Lord, thou art the hearer and answerer of prayer. Thou hast encouraged us to be importunate in prayer. Thou hast assured us that thou art more willing to grant thy Holy Spirit to those who ask thee, than earthly parents are to give good things to their children. O Lord, grant us such blessings as thou seest to be good for us. Thou knowest our wants better than we can explain or express them unto thee. Do thou then suit thy blessings to our need.

O thou, who searchest Jerusalem as with a lighted

candle, do thou search our hearts; see if there be any wicked way in us and lead us in the way everlasting. Lead us not in our own way, but choose thou for us. Let us rejoice in thee as a rich Provider, and an all-wise Provider, who will give us nothing and deny us nothing, but what is for our good.

We commend to thy protection all near and dear to us this night. Keep them, gracious Father, under the shadow of thy wings; bless them in themselves, and make them also a blessing to others. May they never lose sight of the chief end of their being, to glorify thee on earth and enjoy thee forever in heaven. Bless our own family. We thank thee for all thy great goodness in the past. The Lord hath been mindful of us, and he will bless us.

Do good in thy good pleasure unto Zion. Build thou the walls of Jerusalem. May every branch of thy church universal be blest with tokens of thy favor. Revive thy work, O God, in the midst of the years.

Take charge of us this night; it is thou who givest thy beloved sleep; it is thou, Lord, only, who makest us to dwell in safety. Spare us if it be thy will, to see the light, and enjoy the comforts of another day. These and all other blessings we ask for Christ's sake. Amen.

THURSDAY MORNING.

YE are the children of the Lord your God.—Deut. xiv. 1.
One is your Father, which is in heaven.—Matt. xxiii. 9.

Most blessed God, thou hast again permitted us to see
the beginning of a new day. We desire to accept every
new morning as a fresh gift of thy love. We are the constant dependents on thy bounty. If thy sustaining arm be
withdrawn, we instantly perish.

We are unworthy to come into thy presence. Thou
mightest righteously leaves us to perish in our sins, and
make us the monuments of thy displeasure. But in the
midst of wrath thou art remembering unmerited mercy.

We come to thee through the living way of access.
We cast ourselves on the full, free and everlasting salvation
of our adorable Redeemer. Our souls would magnify the
Lord; our spirits would rejoice in God, our Savior, for he
that is mighty hath done great things for us, and holy is his
name. Blessed be the Lord God of Israel, for he hath
visited and redeemed his people. May each of us have a
personal and a saving interest in all those covenant blessings, which he died to purchase, and which he lives to bestow. May we take him as ours only—ours wholly—ours
for every step Zion-ward—ours till we reach the gates of
glory—yea ours for ever and ever.

O Lord, look down in mercy on a world lying in sin
and iniquity; sinners disregard thy law and set at naught
thy commandments, and they grieve the souls of the righteous. O stay the progress of sin, and enlighten the minds
of those who are blinded by Satan, so that they may leave
off from their sins and be converted. We thank thee, our

heavenly Father, that thou hast led us out of the Sodom of sin and the bondage of Satan, and dost daily draw us nearer unto thyself. Strengthen us, therefore, that we may resist all the allurements and temptations of Satan, do thou enable us to rise above the world and all its sinful pleasures. We would cultivate a closer communion with thee, our God and Father, our Lord and Savior. Pour out thy Holy Spirit upon us and sanctify our hearts. Then we shall hate and forsake sin, and love and pursue holiness, without which no man can see God. We rely not on our own strength, but we trust in Christ, whose grace shall be sufficient for us in every time of need.

Bless that branch of thy church with which we are united; bless thy holy church universal. Have mercy on the heathen who are sitting in darkness, who know not thee, the true and living God, and Jesus Christ, the only name given by which we can be saved. May Christ lifted up, by the attraction of his cross draw all men unto him. Hasten the time when no man shall have need to say to his brother, Know thou the Lord, for all shall know him, from the least to the greatest.

Hear us, O Lord, in these our humble and imperfect prayers, for our Redeemer's sake. Amen.

·THURSDAY EVENING.

EVEN so it is not the will of your Father which is in heaven, that one of these little ones should perish.—Matt. xviii. 14.

O Lord God, our heavenly Father, we thank thee that we have been brought safely to the close of this day with no visible marks of thy displeasure upon us. Forgive, O Lord, for Christ's sake, where we have done those things we should not have done, and left undone those things we should have done. Pardon the imperfections of even our best services.

We thank thee that we were not born of heathen parents in a heathen land, where they know not the true God and his Son Jesus Christ, the only name given on earth wherein we can be saved; where they bow down to stocks and stones, dumb idols, the work of their own hands, that can not hear their prayers, nor forgive their sins, nor save their souls, nor give any hope of a blessed life after death. But we thank thee that thou hast given us our birth and education in a christian land, where we have thy holy word, as the revelation of thy will, the light upon our way to heaven; where we have thy church with her sacraments and ordinances of religion; where we have the gospel ministry, and all the means by which we may grow in the grace of God and the knowledge of our Lord and Savior Jesus Christ. O Lord, we would realize that in point of privilege we are exalted to heaven. Help us therefore also to realize our great responsibility, and make a proper use of these means of grace, lest the heathen rise up in Judgment to condemn us.

We rejoice to look back on the way by which thou

hast hitherto led us ; protecting us from danger, supporting us in trouble, dispelling our 'fears, and fulfilling our hopes. We bless thee for our creation, for our preservation, and for all the blessings of this life; but above all, for thine inestimable gift, Jesus, the Son of thy love. May Jesus say to us, as he did to the believing suppliant of old, " Your sins are forgiven you : go in peace." We would seek to draw fresh supplies from the fountain of his grace ; knowing that there is a fullness in him to meet all our wants and minister to all our necessities.

It is our desire, O heavenly Father, to leave ourselves entirely in thy hands. Whether prosperity or adversity come to us, whether thou chasten or gladden us, O bring us nearer to thyself. Save us from the bitterest of all trials, the removal of thy love, the loss of thy favor. Strengthen us for duty ; guard us from temptation ; and enable us to pass through things temporal, that finally we lose not the things that are eternal.

We pray for thy cause and kingdom everywhere. Give thy Son the heathen for his inheritance, and the uttermost parts of the earth for his possession. May he take to himself his great power and reign. May there soon be voices heard saying, " The kingdoms of this world are become the one kingdom of our Lord and his Christ."

O Lord, take the charge of us this night during the unconscious hours of sleep; may we be strengthened by sleep and rest for the duties of the coming day, if it is thy holy will that we shall see its returning light. We ask all for Christ's sake. Amen.

FRIDAY MORNING.

I N the fear of the Lord is strong confidence : and his children shall
have a place of refuge.—Prov. xiv. 26.

Our Father who art in heaven, what are we, sinful dust
and ashes, that we should be permitted, morning after morning, to take thy name upon our lips! We bless thee for all
the unnumbered proofs of thy kindness. From our earliest
years we have been the recipients of thy bounty. With a
Father's tenderness thou hast watched over us. Surely,
goodness and mercy have followed us all the days of our lives,

O Lord, thou art a sun and shield, our consolation,
our portion and our exceeding great reward. We need not
be afraid, though heaven and earth should pass away, for
thou hast given us thy Son, thine only begotten Son, who
has secured for us the inheritance of the heavenly Canaan.
Thou couldest have given us nothing more precious, nothing more glorious. For when we have Christ dwelling in
us, the hope of glory, then we have that which can make
us eternally happy. But what words can express the debt
of gratitude which we owe to thee, or what return can we
make to thee for thine infinite love? All that we have we
have received from thee, and all that we hope to enjoy we
must receive from thy hand. We have nothing that we can
strictly call our own, but our sins. Lord cleanse us from
our sins through the atoning blood of Christ. Sanctify our
hearts and make them fit temples for the indwelling of thy
Holy Spirit. We would dedicate ourselves, soul and body,
as a living sacrifice, wholly and acceptable to thee. And
when the sun of our lives shall go down and the darkness
of death shall gather around us, then do thou let us depart

in peace, and resign our souls into thy hands, through Jesus Christ our Savior.

O Lord, we adore thee as God over all, blessed for evermore. Thou art the former of our bodies and the Father of our spirits; the God in whom we live and move and have our being. O give us grateful hearts; feeling that the least blesing we enjoy, is unmerited on our part, and a gift of free grace on thine.

We come anew, glorying in the work and merits of our adorable Redeemer. Thou art in him waiting to be gracious, not willing that any should perish. May our eye of faith be kept, blessed Savior, constantly on thee and thy completed salvation. We have nothing to pay, thou hast *paid* all. We have nothing to procure, thou hast *procured* all; everlasting forgiveness, everlasting righteousnes, union and communion with thee, now and ever more. To thee we look for everything. Save us from every false confidence. Elevate our affections; purify our desires; make us more heavenly minded. Let us while living in the world, live above it. Let thy Spirit be our teacher; let thy word be our guide; let thy will be our controlling motive; let thy glory be our ultimate end. May we make religion more the one thing needful. Let us not remain content with an indefinate hope of final safety. Pilgrims and strangers on earth, may we declare plainly, that we seek a better country. We put ourselves, blessed God, into thy hands this day. May all our doings this day, begun, carried on, and ended in thee, redound, through Jesus Christ, to thy praise and glory. Amen.

FRIDAY EVENING.

I WILL be a Father unto you, and ye shall be my sons and daughters, saith the Lord Almighty.—2 Cor. vi. 18.

O holy Lord God! How wonderful are thy ways. As the heavens are higher than the earth, so are thy thoughts higher than our thoughts. We cannot always comprehend thine inscrutable dealings, but we know that thou doest all things well. O help us to have at least some faint conception of the length and the breadth, the height and the depth of the love of God in Christ Jesus, which passeth all human knowledge and understanding.

O God, our Father, who art in heaven, we thank thee for the gift of thy Son, who came into the world to seek and to save lost sinners, who fulfilled the whole law by a life of perfect obedience, who in the days of his ministry went about doing good to the bodies and souls of men, who gave us the most perfect rules of life and conduct, who enlightened the world with truth and wisdom from heaven, and then died on the cross for our sins. And we thank thee not only for a Savior who was crucified, dead and buried, but for a Savior that liveth again, having risen from the dead for our justification and ascended to heaven, where he intercedeth for us, and where he hath prepared a place for us in the mansions of our heavenly Father's house, whence he will come again and receive us to himself, that where he is, we may be also. O help us to embrace this almighty Savior by a living faith, and finally may we be received by him into that house not made with hands, whose builder and maker is God.

Enable us to feel our sins—to have a deep and heartfelt consciousness of their odiousness in thy sight. Give us grace in true penitence and contrition of heart to cast ourselves, *un*worthy as we are, on the infinite worthiness of him who is *all*worthy. For his sake receive us graciously and love us freely. We rejoice to think on the love which he had for us from all eternity. We rejoice to know that it is the same at this day, that it was then ; unchanging, everlasting. O thou great High Priest who hast entered within the veil, where thou art interceding for us, do thou recieve our prayers and present them at the mercy seat. O thou Holy Spirit, proceeding from the Father and the Son, sanctify us, body, soul and spirit. Make us altogether what thou wouldst have us to be. Let us be willing, if need be, to deny ourselves and take up our cross and follow thee.

God of Bethel, thou God of all the families of the earth, who hast promised to show mercy to thousands of them that love thee, do thou bless our family, and give us the heritage of those who love thy name. Let none of us be left to seek for the first time a living Savior at a dying hour. But laying hold on him now, may we be found at last unto praise and honor and glory at his appearing and in his kingdom.

We would retire to rest this night, reposing on thy gracious providence, beseeching thee, if it be thy will, to spare us to see the light and to enjoy the comforts of a new day ; and all we ask is in the name and for the sake of Jesus Christ our only Savior. Amen.

SATURDAY MORNING.

G RACE be to you, and peace, from God our Father, and from the
    Lord Jesus Christ.—Eph. i. 2.

Almighty God, we come again this morning into thy
sacred presence.   Glory be to thy holy name that we have
access to the throne of grace.   Anew we draw near to the
open fountain; anew, gracious Savior, we plead thy precious blood.   Thine own wondrous love brought thee from
thy throne in heaven to proclaim liberty to the captives and
the opening of the prison to them that are bound.   What
shall we render unto thee for all thy kindness to us, and
what can we give unto thee for thy boundless love?   All
we can do is to give ourselves to thee, soul and body.
    O Lord Jesus, who in the days of thy ministry on earth
didst go about doing good to the bodies and souls of men,
help us to imitate thy holy example, as far as possible to
follow thee in all thine imitable perfections.   Let thy Spirit
dwell richly in our hearts, that we may be like thee in loving our fellow men and laboring to do them good in body
and soul.   May we also have his forgiving Spirit, who could
pray even for his enemies and murderers, " Father, forgive
them, they know not what they do."   And as Jesus sent
forth his apostles as missionaries to preach the Gospel to a
benighted and sinful world, so may we also feel it to be our
duty to help send the glorious Gospel of salvation to the
benighted heathen, who know nothing of thee, the only true
and living God, and thee, O thou blessed Savior, who hast
wrought out a perfect redemption for all mankind.
    We would look away from ourselves, to thy dear Son,
our Redeemer; feeling, that if we are saved it must be by

him alone. May he be formed within us the hope of glory. By his grace and Spirit may we be brought under the power and influence of renewed affections. Let us seek to manifest the reality of our union with him, by adorning the doctrine of God our Savior in our daily walk and conversation. May ours be an active and devoted obedience. Expel from us whatever is unholy. Let us live as the expectants of a glorious immortality. Lord, may we habitually remember, that here we are pilgrims. O be thou our constant guide in all our journeys. Let us never go, but where thou directest; let us never hesitate when and where thou callest us. May we feel that all the circumstances of life—its joys and its sorrows, its comforts and crosses, are ordained by thee in adorable wisdom. Our way might have been hedged up with thorns, but it has been full of mercy. Thou hast been our help, leave us not, nor forsake us, O God of our salvation. Give us to see written over every hour of the future, " So shall thy strength be."

Bless all near and dear to us. Defend our friends by thy mighty power. Surround them with thy favor as with a wall, and bring them at last to the enjoyment of thine immediate presence. Bless especially those of us now before thee. May we all be objects of thy love, and subjects of thy grace; may we be enabled to say, Our Father, thou shalt be the guide of our lives.

We commend each and all of us this day to thy keeping. Let us enter upon its duties with our souls staid on thee. And all that we ask is in the name and for the sake of the Lord Jesus Christ, to whom with thee and the Holy Spirit be all honor and glory, world without end. Amen.

SATURDAY EVENING.

LIKE as a father pitieth his children, so the Lord pitieth them that fear him.—Ps. ciii. 13.

O Lord, we thank thee, that thou hast brought us in safety to the close of another day and the end of another week. Hitherto the Lord hath helped us. We are unworthy of the least of thy mercies. If thou hadst dealt with us as we have deserved, or judged us according to our sins, we could not answer thee for one of a thousand.

O Lord, thy favor is life. Nothing but the enjoyment of thine infinite love can satisfy the longings of our souls. Whom have we in heaven, O God, but thee? and there is none upon earth we would desire beside thee. We would call upon our souls to praise the Lord, and all that is within us to bless his holy name, who forgiveth all our sins, who healeth all our diseases, and crowneth us with loving kindness.

How merciful and gracious art thou, our God and Father, for having opened up a way to heaven by the mission of thy Son Jesus Christ into the world, that whosoever believeth on him should not perish, but have eternal life. We are pilgrims and strangers on earth as our fathers were. We have no abiding city here, but we seek a better country, the heavenly Canaan, which is to be the eternal inheritance of thy people. Help us to press forward with diligence and zeal in our pilgrimage towards heaven, our eternal home, looking toward the prize of our high calling in Christ Jesus our Lord. We would raise a memorial, upon the altars of our hearts, and bring ourselves and all we have and are as a living sacrifice, reasonable and acceptable to thee. O

Lord, receive us graciously and love us freely for the sake of thy Son, our Lord and Savior Jesus Christ.

We plead anew Christ's finished atonement. We would glory in nothing but his cross. Help each of us to enjoy the blessedness of the assurance, that there is no condemnation to them that are in Christ Jesus. Let us not rest, until with personal appropriating faith, we can say, " We know whom we have believed, and we are persuaded that he is able to keep that which we have committed unto him."

May thy Holy Spirit take of the things that are Christ's and show them unto our souls. May he touch us as with a live coal from off the altar ; purifying our affections, elevating our desires ; making our hearts living temples, with this as their inscription, " Holiness unto the Lord."

Bless our beloved friends both near and at a distance ; may they all be near to thee. May there be no separation between them and thy favor. Any who may be sick, Lord, heal them ; any who are in bereavement, Lord, comfort them.

Pity the careless, ungodly world—stop the spread of impiety ; establish the reign of purity and righteousness. Give us grace to be faithful among the faithless ; resolving, that whatever others do, as for us, we will serve the Lord.

Be with us this night ; watch over us while we sleep. May night after night of refreshing slumber be to us the emblem of that better rest above, when in perfect peace we shall dwell in the house of the Lord forever. Prepare us for the services of the coming Sabbath day. Attune our minds for its sacred duties. May each returning Sabbath, as it brings us nearer to eternity, find us better prepared for heaven and its unalloyed happiness. And all that we ask is for the Redeemer's sake. Amen.

SUNDAY MORNING.

Y OUR Father knoweth what things ye have need of before ye ask
him.—Matt. vi. 8.

O God, our heavenly Father, we thank thee for the
undisturbed repose and the refreshing sleep granted us during the past night. It is owing to thy paternal care over
us that we have passed the night in safety, and once more
awake to enter on the enjoyments of thy holy day.
Blessed be thy holy name for the appointment of this day
of bodily rest and spiritual communion with thee, our God
and Father. We thank thee for thy church, for the ministry
of the gospel, for thy holy word and all the means of grace.
Give us a desire for spiritual blessings, a hunger and a
thirst after righteousness, and may the Holy Spirit impress
the truth upon our hearts and enlighten us with wisdom
from on high.

When we meet in the congregation of thy people be
thou with us there; for thou hast promised to be with thy
church to the end of time, and wherever thy people meet
in thy name, thou wilt be in the midst of them. May we
and all with whom we shall worship, realize thy presence,
and feel that it was good for us to be there, because the
Savior was in the midst of us and we felt him precious to
our souls. Give us a reverencial and godly fear when we
are in thy house. Strengthen our faith, increase our love
and revive all our spiritual graces. When we sing, may we
praise thee in our *hearts*, and sing with the spirit and the
understanding. When we unite in the words of prayer,
may it not be a mere lip service, but may we worship thee
in spirit and in truth. Enlighten our understanding to

receive thy word. Speak thou to us this day by thy Word and by thy Spirit. May we have the hearing ear, the understanding mind, the applying conscience, the feeling heart, and the earnest disposition to carry out in our lives the holy doctrines of the religion which we profess.

Be with all those who shall minister in thy holy sanctuary this day. Fill them with thy Holy Spirit, and as they labor to teach others, may they themselves be taught of thee. Endue them with power from on high; give them an ardent zeal for the salvation of sinners; take away from them all slavish fear of man, and all selfish desire for the praise of men, but give them a single eye to the glory of God.

Look in compassion on the heathen, who are sitting in spiritual darkness and the shadow of death, who worship idols, the work of their own hands and who have never heard of Christ, the Savior of the world; look in mercy on the Jews who still reject the Messiah that came to save them; look in mercy on all atheists and infidels, both at home and abroad. Oh, send out thy light and thy truth among the people. Give power and efficacy to thy preached gospel everywhere and let not thy word return unto thee void.

All through this day may we have sweet communion with thee our Father who art in heaven. Be with us in private as well as in public; help us to guard our words and our thoughts and to keep near to thee in our hearts.

Grant thy special grace and blessing to our relatives and friends; those who are at home with us and those who are far away. Make this day to them also, as well as to us a day of peace and joy, and may we and they meet in spirit before the throne of grace.

Hear us in our feeble prayers for our Savior's sake. Amen.

SUNDAY EVENING.

NEITHER can they die any more: for they are equal unto the angels; and are the children of God, being the children of the resurrection.—Luke xx. 36.

O Lord God, our Father who art in heaven, again we come to thee in our Redeemer's name, and we would close the holy Sabbath day with prayer and praise.

We thank thee for this day of sacred rest. We thank thee for one day in seven, on which we can rest from our bodily labors, and engage in those services which shall fit us for that heavenly rest, prepared for thy redeemed people, where congregations ne'er break up, and Sabbaths have no end. We thank thee for every spiritual desire that we have felt for communion with thee, and for every spiritual thought that passed through our minds; for every devout feeling that has affected our hearts we give praise to thee; for all these came from thee, all were the gift and work of thy gracious Spirit within us.

Let us not have heard thy word to-day in vain. Deepen its impression on our hearts; help us to remember it and treasure it up in our minds, and live and walk by its light. May it indeed be a light to our path and a lamp to our feet on our way to heaven.

Forgive where we have come short. Pardon the sins even of our best services. If our minds have wandered in worship, if we have forgotten that we were in thy holy presence, if light and vain thoughts have crept into our religious meditations, if there has been any lack of serious and earnest attention to thy word, forgive us for the Redeemer's sake. May we be more watchful in future; may his precious blood cleanse us from every stain of sin, and may we lie down to rest at peace with God and man.

To thy tender care we now commend ourselves and all whom we love. May thy peace be with us all. Watch over us through the night and shield us from harm, both temporal and spiritual. May our last thought e'er we close our eyes in sleep, be of thee, our Father in heaven, and of thee our dear Savior, and may our first thoughts on waking, also turn to thee our Creator, our Redeemer, our bountiful Benefactor and our Friend.

We pray for any who specially stand in need of our prayers; for those in spiritual darkness, surrounded by many temptations; for those laid on beds of sickness and pain; for those passing through the valley and shadow of death; for those mourning their "loved and lost" ones. Grant them the consolations of religion, and help them to be resigned to thy will, saying, Even so Father, for so it seems good in thy sight.

The Lord bless us and keep us;

The Lord make his face to shine upon us, and be gracious unto us;

The Lord lift up his countenance upon us, and give us peace;

The grace of our Lord Jesus Christ be with us all. Amen.

MONDAY MORNING.

I WILL cause them to walk by the rivers of waters in a straight way, wherein they shall not stumble: for I am a father to Israel, and Ephraim is my first-born.—Jer. xxxi. 9.

Gracious God, our heavenly Father, thou hast heard our prayers and kept us safe through the night. And now we wake again in health and peace to praise and magnify thy name.

We are entering upon the duties and labors of another day. We are dependent upon thee for all things by day as well as by night. We need thy protecting care whether we wake or sleep. Bless us also this day; guide, uphold and defend us. Graciously supply all our wants; give us thy Holy Spirit; keep us under the shadow of thy wing, and help us in all that we do, whether we eat or drink, or whatsoever we do, to do all to the glory of thy name.

We are weak; be thou our strength. We are blind and ignorant; may thy word be a lamp to our feet and a light to our path. We know not what this day may bring forth; but thou knowest and orderest all things. Heavenly Father, this is our comfort, that we are in thy hands, and that thou wilt never leave or forsake those who put their trust in thee. Increase our faith, enable us to trust in thee more fully and constantly; keep us ever near to thee and we shall be safe.

Bless us as a household. Cause us to dwell together in harmony and love. May there be no envy or ill will among us, no anger or strife; may no unkind word this day pass our lips; make us to love each other as brethren and sisters in thought and word and deed. May we be helpers to each other, and not hinderers in our spiritual life; and should any provocation be received, incline our hearts and enable us to be merciful, forbearing and forgiving.

Help us to remember and put to practice the lesson of instruction and admonition on the Lord's day; may we be not only hearers but also doers of thy word. We desire to begin the day with thee, and when we go out from this family altar to our various employments for the day, give us grace in all our intercourse or business with others to behave as Christians, and to bring no dishonor on thy name.

Bless our land and nation; may it be a land as much distinguished for the morality and Christian piety of its inhabitants, as it is for its civil and religious privileges. Stay the progress of vice and ungodliness, of drunkenness and crime, of Sabbath desecration and wickedness of every kind; and grant that true religion may increase and abound among us more and more.

Especially, we pray thee, bless the youth in our churches and Sunday-schools. Shield the young from temptation of the flesh, the world and the devil; it is upon them as the future members of the church that her spiritual condition and prosperity must depend.

These and all other needful blessings we humbly ask in the name and for the sake of Jesus Christ thy Son our Lord. Amen.

MONDAY EVENING.

EVEN so, Father; for so it seemed good in thy sight.—Luke x. 21.

Give ear, O Lord, to our prayer, and attend to the voice of our supplications; hear us in this our evening prayer for our Savior's sake.

We thank thee for the mercies thou hast again bestowed upon us. Another day has come and gone, and thou hast not forgotten us, or overlooked our wants. Thou hast in thy bounty given us all that we need, and hast preserved us in life and health and safety. Here we will raise our Ebenezer, for hitherto the Lord hath helped us.

We come to implore forgiveness for our sins. Let not one unpardoned sin remain upon us this night. Pardon all that our own conscience tells us has been wrong, and all our sins and short comings of which we ourselves are unconscious, but which have all been seen and known of thee.

Grant us grace to learn from our own faults and failings. If some old temptation has beset us and we have fallen, O give us a contrite heart and a deeply humbled spirit. Yet suffer us not to despair; help us to feel more our own weakness, and to look to thee alone for grace and strength. Help us to be more watchful in the future than we have been in the past. Give us strength from on high. May thy Holy Spirit prevail within us, and subdue everything that is evil and wrong.

May that peace which the Savior promised to his disciples be ours, may that peace which passeth all understanding be ours in a larger measure. Heavenly Father, suffer not our hearts to be troubled or afraid. Keep us always in peace and confidence, and help us daily to walk in the Spirit. Bless thy holy word more and more to us, help us to search the Scriptures, for they testify of Jesus, and make us wise unto salvation. May the Holy Scriptures be circulated to the ends of the earth. May thy written and thy preached word be the means of turning many from darkness unto light; may it be to many hearts the power of God unto salvation. Have mercy upon those to whom it has come, but who have rejected it and refuse to be enlightened by its heavenly truths. Look in mercy upon the unbelievers, the scoffers and despisers of thy word in our own and other lands.

Bless our beloved friends wherever they are. Do thou hallow every earthly tie by making it a heavenly one. May they all be the children of God by faith in Jesus Christ. Bind up the broken hearts; grant rest to the weary, a home to the homeless, be thou a father to the orphans and a husband to the widow. May those appointed unto death be prepared for the great change.

Amid the uncertainties of life may we be so living and walking by the active faith in a living Savior, that when that solemn hour of our departure from earth shall come, we may have nothing to do, but to die and wake up in glory everlasting.

And now, our heavenly Father, take us and all that are dear to us into thy care for the night and may thy blessing abide upon us while we sleep, for the sake of Jesus Christ, our Savior. Amen.

TUESDAY MORNING.

IF ye, then, being evil, know how to give good gifts unto your children, how much more shall your Father which is in heaven give good things to them that ask him?—Matt. vii. 11.

O Lord God, our Father who art in heaven. Heaven is thy throne and the earth is thy footstool, angels and archangels veil their faces before thee and cry out, holy, holy, holy, art thou Lord God of hosts, heaven and earth are full of thy glory.

We who are the dwellers upon thy footstool beseech thee to look down upon us with favor and loving kindness for our Redeemer's sake. We are not worthy to come into thy presence; but we come not in our own name or righteousness; we come in his name who is the living way and for whose sake thou wilt recieve all who come to thee in true penitence and faith.

We give thee thanks for the knowledge of Jesus Christ, who came into the world to save lost sinners. We thank thee that we have been taught in thy word that he is an all-sufficient Savior, able to save, and as willing as he is able to save to the uttermost, all who come to thee through him. We thank thee for a Savior who not only died to atone for our sins, but who rose from the dead and liveth again, ready to bestow those blessings which he purchased by his precious blood. We thank thee for the gift of the Holy Ghost, whose office it is to teach, and comfort and sanctify us. We thank thee for the hope of eternal life through Jesus Christ.

Help us this day to walk by faith. As thou hast shielded us through the night, so we pray thee to protect us through this day. Prepare us for whatever may be in store for us. Make us watchful and prayerful. Whatever our hands find to do this day, may we do it with our might.

And now we thank thee for the temporal blessings we enjoy; for food and raiment, for health and strength of body and of mind, for our civil liberty, for our birth and education in a Christian land. May we never forget that all these things are bestowed upon us by thy bountiful hand.

Oh Lord our heavenly Father, how uncertain is our life in this world; every day brings us nearer to the end of our earthly pilgrimage; may we therefore be every day better prepared for the enjoyments of the bliss of heaven which is to be our eternal home. Grant that amidst earth's changes our hearts may be fixed upon that home, where there are true, pure and permanent joys. May the main tendency of our hearts be heavenward. May our treasures be laid up in heaven and may our hearts be there. O grant us grace to consider no burden too heavy to be borne; no cross too bitter to be endured, and no foe too fierce to be met, so that we may do all that thou wouldst have us to do, so that we may be made worthy partakers of the inheritance of the saints in light, so that at last an abundant entrance may be ministered unto us into Christ's everlasting kingdom.

And now we commend unto thy fatherly care our loved ones, both those who are present with us here, and those who are far away; protect and shield them by thine almighty arm from all danger; may no harm come near them and no danger befall them, but keep them safely under the shadow of thy wings, and unto the Father, Son and Holy Ghost, be all honor and praise, world without end. Amen.

TUESDAY EVENING.

NOT for that nation only, but that also he should gather together in one the children of God that were scattered abroad.—John xi. 52.

O Lord our God, we draw near this evening to the throne of grace. We thank thee for thy care over us during the past day. We thank thee for the goodness and mercy that have followed us during this day. While others have been in want of food to sustain their lives, our table has been loaded with plenty; while others have met with accidents or misfortunes, thou hast kept us, as it were, under the hollow of thy hand, and hast permitted no harm to befall us; while others have been laid on beds of sickness and pain, we have been kept in health of body and mind. O, may our lives, preserved by thy bounty, be dedicated to thy praise.

But far above all thine other gifts we bless thee for the gift of thine only Son, our Lord Jesus Christ, for the redemption which he has wrought out for us, for the means of grace and for the hope of glory. We bless thee that Jesus Christ has brought in an everlasting righteousness; that he has fulfilled the whole law and made it honorable; that he has dispelled the darkness of the valley of death, and opened the gates of heaven to all believers.

We acknowledge our sins and unworthiness before thee. Help us to see ourselves as thou seest us. Unveil to us our secret pride. Help us to realize the depths of our natural depravity; and our proneness to sin. Let us see the vileness of sin in view of the cross of Christ. May the power of sin become weaker and weaker in our hearts, and may the power of thy grace within us grow stronger and stronger. Deliver us from our besetting sins. May our souls become holy altars and our bodies living sacrifices, by consecrating ourselves to thy service as instruments of righteousness unto holiness, in newness of spirit.

Bless the aged ; may thy favor and love rest on the hoary heads as a crown of glory. Bless the young ; may they early know what are the only ways of pleasantness and paths of peace. Bless the afflicted, the bereaved, the poor and the dying; may they know him, who hath said, " I will never leave thee, nor forsake thee."

Give us all grace to trust thee at all times and in all thy dealings with us, even when they are contrary to our own wishes or expectations. Let us at all times be enabled to say from our hearts, " Thy will be done ; " and help us to obey thy will above all others. Following thy guiding footsteps, may we say, " The Lord is our shepherd, we shall not want.".

Watch over us, blessed Lord, this night. May thy good angels encamp round about us. Give us, if it please thee, refreshing sleep and undisturbed repose ; may we lie down to rest in thy fear, and awake in thy favor.

Now unto him who is the Creator and Upholder of heaven and earth, who is the King of kings and Lord of lords, who only hath immortality, dwelling in the light which no man can approach unto, whom no man hath seen nor can see, be honor, and power, and glory, and dominion, world without end. Amen.

WEDNESDAY MORNING.

TRULY our fellowship is with the Father, and with his Son Jesus
Christ.—1 John i. 3.

O Lord God almighty, thou Maker, Upholder, and
Judge of all. Seraphim and cherubim adore thee; angels
and archangels worship thee, and cry out, Holy, holy, holy
is the Lord of hosts, heaven and earth are full of thy glory.
We, who are also the creatures of thy hands and the
dependents on thy bounty, would also join with saints and
angels in worshiping and praising thee.

We approach thee as our covenant God and Father,
trusting in the name and merits of our adorable Redeemer.
O what a mercy it is that we have such a perfect and all-
sufficient Savior, who is able and willing to save all who
will come to him in humility, penitence and faith. We
thank thee that " Jesus Christ came into the world to save
sinners," and his invitation still holds good, " Come unto
me all ye who are heavy laden, and I will give you rest for
your souls." We renounce all dependence on ourselves.
We are, in our natural state, spiritually wretched, poor,
blind, and naked, but we take Jesus Christ as all our hope
for time and eternity, all our hope, all our salvation, and all
our desire.

We are no judges of what is good for us ; what blessings are best for us to receive, what mercies thou seest best
to withhold from us. But we rejoice in the infinite wisdom
and goodness of thy dealings with us. May we seek in
every providence to hear thy voice, in every event to read
thy will. May our hearts overflow with love to thee. May
we feel thy favor lightening every cross, and lessening

every care. Lord, give us more of a childlike disposition, which takes God at his word, and delights to do his will. Keep us from pride and vain glory; from envy and unkindness; from all that would exalt us at the expense of others. May we learn to love our neighbor as ourselves.

Look in great mercy on those who are in sorrow or distress; be their support and consolation, and teach us all in the midst of health and strength, to prepare for the time of adversity. We have no abiding city here; time is bearing us on to eternity. May we know what it is to look to a strong tower which can not be shaken. We are in our true rest if we are at peace with thee. Do thou gladden our pathway through life. May we be lighted through the dark valley by the lamp of thy love; and enjoy in heaven and through eternity thy presence and behold thy glory.

God of Bethel, bless our family and all related to us by whatever tie. May they all have a saving interest in the everlasting covenant. Bless the young. O, thou great shepherd of the sheep, preserve them from the snares of a world lying in wickedness. May they be taught of God, and thus inherit thine own promise. " Those who seek me early shall find me."

Take us under thy care this day. May all our duties be gladdened with a sense of thy presence and love. May we have a single eye in all we think and say and do to the honor and glory of thy name, through Jesus Christ our Lord. Amen.

WEDNESDAY EVENING.

THAT ye may be blameless and harmless, the sons of God, without rebuke, in the midst of a crooked and perverse nation, among whom ye shine as lights in the world.—Phil. ii. 15.

O, thou eternal and everlasting God, thou fountain of all happiness, and Father of all our mercies, we desire to express the gratitude of our hearts for all the blessings we have enjoyed this day. Thou hast made our cup to overflow. From our earliest infancy thou hast been our Protector and our guardian. Thou hast shielded us from unknown dangers; from sickness thou hast restored us to health; thou hast filled our hearts with gladness; and in the hour of temptation thou hast kept us from falling. No earthly friend could have loved us and cared for us as thou hast done.

We bless thee, that at all times we have access to the throne of grace. We can come to thee as children to a father, express our varied wants, ask for the pardon of our sins and grace to help in every time of need. Thou hast all the treasures of divine grace; giving does not impoverish thee and withholding does not enrich thee. And thou hast declared thyself more willing to give thy Holy Spirit to those who ask thee in Christ's name, than earthly parents are willing to give good things to their children.

Do thou, then, our Heavenly Father, grant us those things which thou seest we need, and which thou knowest to be good for us.

By nature we are helpless, hopeless; but we cast ourselves on him, who is the help, and hope, and friend of all who trust in him. We have no trust, but in his wondrous work. Take away our sins, cleanse our hearts by his precious blood. Sanctify us by thy Holy Spirit. Draw us near to thee, that we may be able to exclaim, "Who shall separate us from the love of Christ?" Draw us, O Lord, nearer and nearer to thee. May every thought and feeling and temper be brought into obedience to Jesus. May we love what he loves and hate what he hates. May we know the happiness of true holiness, and experience somewhat the joy of angels in doing thy holy will on earth as they do it in heaven. Fill us with all joy and peace in believing, that we may abound in hope through the power of the Holy Ghost.

Bless our family and friends; may our household be one of the dwellings of the righteous. May every member of it be zealous in the promotion of thy glory, remembering that the day is coming, when we shall be called upon to give an account for the deeds done in the body.

Our days and nights are passing away and bearing their records with them to the Judgment bar. Let us be living with our final account always in view. Forbid that any of us should be found seeking oil when the lamp of life is going out. Let us die daily to sin and live daily to God; that when the hour of our earthly departure comes, it may be to all of us the birthday of a new life, in glory everlasting.

We ask all these blessings in the name and for the sake of our adorable Redeemer, who is now within the veil, where, with thee, O eternal Father; and thee, O ever blessed comforter, three in one, in covenant for our redemption, who ever liveth and reigneth, world without end. Amen.

THURSDAY MORNING.

BELOVED, now are we the sons of God, and it doth not yet appear what we shall be: but we know that, when he shall appear, we shall be like him; for we shall see him as he is.—1 John iii. 2.

O Lord God, our Heavenly Father, another day has in mercy dawned upon us. We desire to enter on its every duty with our minds stayed on thee. May all our doings be in accordance with thy will, so that we may be enabled to do those things that are pleasing in thy sight, and promote the glory of thy holy name.

We bless thee especially for Jesus and his great salvation. We rejoice that he is both willing and able, and as willing as he is able, to save unto the uttermost; that all are alike invited and welcome to come to the fountain, which Jesus has opened for sin and uncleanness, wherein they can wash and be clean.

Lord, help us to improve the many privileges which we have. May we faithfully use the means of grace, for our own growth in holiness and a consistent walk and conversation in the world. May this be our habitual feeling—" What manner of persons ought we to be in all holy conversation and godliness ? "

We commend to thy fatherly care all those who are distressed and afflicted. Take them under thy special protection. Let thy suffering people wait till they hear the " still small voice " speaking comfort and consolation to their souls. Calling upon thee in the day of trouble, and receiving help from thee, may they be led to " glorify thee in the midst of their afflictions."

Teach us all in the time of health and strength so to

live, that when the night of death comes we may be enabled to say, "Now, Lord, lettest thou thy servant depart in peace."

Bless our beloved friends ; forbid that any one of them should be found wanting on the day when thou makest up thy jewels. May they all be set as gems in Emanuels crown, and be found unto praise and honor and glory, at his second coming.

Bless that branch of thy church with which we are so intimately united. Bless thy church universal. Imbue her ministers and people with the sanctifying influence of thy Holy Spirit. Extend everywhere the borders of the Redeemer's Kingdom. The harvest truly is plenteous and the laborers are few. We would pray the Lord of the harvest to send forth laborers, and incline the hearts of Christian people to pray for the missionaries in heathen lands, and support them in their labors by liberal contributions.

Be thou with us this day. May thine everlasting arms be beneath and around us for good; may we be diligent in business, fervent in spirit, serving the Lord; and we will look forward with joyful hearts to that better world, where we shall be always of the same mind with thee, when we shall be *with* thee, and *like* thee; serving thee without distraction; and where sin and sorrow shall be no more felt or dreaded. And unto thee, Father, Son, and Holy Ghost, shall be all the glory, world without end. Amen.

THURSDAY EVENING.

YE are all the children of God by faith in Christ Jesus.—Gal. iii. 26.

O Lord, our God, we come into thy sacred presence this evening again to thank thee for thy protection and care over us during the day. On thee we are dependent for every temporal blessing, and every spiritual privilege we enjoy. If we have this day been enabled to overcome temptation, and fight against sin, it is thy grace which has enabled us to do so. We are weak, but thou art strong; protect us ever by thine almighty arm against all temporal and spiritual harm; if thou art for us, no one can be successfully against us.

O Lord God of heaven and earth, we magnify thy majesty and greatness in thine unfathomable and infinite love for sinners! Thou didst not punish fallen and rebellious sinners, but thou didst send thine only begotten Son to die on the cross for them, as a ransom from their guilt. We adore thee for thine unspeakable love in giving thy dear Son, to become sin for us, in order that we poor, miserable sinners might obtain that righteousness which avails in thy presence. That is thy greatness, that thou dost hear the sinner in thine infinite love, seek him, and care for him, to save and make him happy. Thou Lord Jesus, givest us thy pierced hand, which has imparted to us so much love, that we must stand ashamed as we contemplate it, and our eyes be bathed in tears full of praise and gratitude.

And while we look by simple faith to the glorious atonement of Christ, as the only ground of our justification, we would look to the Holy Spirit to work in us all the good pleasure of his will, enabling us to walk and to act in obedience to thy holy commandments. Lord, give us supreme love to thee ; fervent charity to all men ; faithfulness to every trust confided to our hands. May we seek to live as we would wish we had been living, when we come to die.

Have mercy on the sons and daughters of sorrow, let them own thy hand in all their afflictions ; let them rest in thy love ; let them rejoice in him who " hath borne our griefs and carried our sorrows ;" and if they see not the bright light in the cloud, may they trust thine own promise, " At evening time it shall be light."

Advance thy cause and kingdom in the world. Pour out upon thy ministers, and missionaries, and churches the healthful Spirit of thy grace. May the time soon come when all the ends of the earth shall see the salvation of God.

Bless our own family and household, and all that are nearest and dearest to us. May the peace of God, which passeth understanding, keep their hearts. Number them with thy saints in glory everlasting.

Be with us through this night. May our bodies be refreshed by sleep ; and may we awake to the duties of a new day with our minds stayed on thee. And unto thy great name, Father, Son, and Holy Spirit, we ascribe all blessing, and honor, and glory, and praise, now and forever. Amen.

FRIDAY MORNING.

THIS my Son was dead, and is alive again; he was lost, and is found.—Luke xv. 24.

Our Father, who art in heaven, we draw near in the name of him whom thou hearest always. "Nothing in our hands we bring,"—we would cling "simply to his cross." Empty us of all self-righteousness;—let us feel our deep creature-destitution;—let us stand alone in the finished righteousness of the All-righteous One. We have forfeited all claim to thy favor, and if we had been left to our own treacherous hearts and wayward wills, we must long ago have perished.

We desire to look to thy grace in the future. There is not a corruption we have within us which that grace is unable to subdue; there is not a cross, or trial, or care, but it will enable us to endure. Whatever thy dealings may be, let us cheerfully confide in their wisdom and faithfulness. We are poor judges of what is good for us, but we can trust thee in all things;—in what is great and what is small, what is dark and what is bright, what is joyous and what is grievous. We rejoice that all is in thy hands, and all is for the best. May we ever regard sin as our greatest trial. When temptation assails us, grant us power to resist it. May our conversation, our tempers, our affections, our desires, be regulated by the example of our divine Lord and Master. Give us his meekness of spirit, which no provocation could ruffle,—his forgiveness of injuries amid ingratitude and scorn,—his calm, unmurmuring submission to thy holy will.

Bless all the sons and daughters of affliction. Let

them view every dark providence as an errand of love in disguise;—a messenger sent from the eternal throne, to minister to them who are heirs of salvation. May we all live as pilgrims on the earth. Make us meet for the time when our earthly work and warfare shall cease, and when, in unspotted sanctity, we shall stand without fault before thy throne.

The Lord bless our neighbors, and show us how to do them good. Help us at all times to strive to be a blessing to their bodies and their souls, and may they be a blessing to us. Bless those of them who call upon thy name. And have mercy upon such as know thee not, neither worship nor serve thee. Turn their hearts to the Savior and their feet to thy commandments.

Lord, take the charge of each and all of us. Keep us this day without sin. May all our doings be ordered by thy governance, to do that which is well-pleasing in thy sight, through Jesus Christ our only Lord and Savior. Amen.

FRIDAY EVENING.

BLESSED be God, even the Father of our Lord Jesus Christ, the Father of mercies, and the God of all comfort; who comforteth us in all our tribulation.—2 Cor. i. 3, 4.

O God, we desire to draw near into thy sacred presence, thanking thee for the mercies granted us during another day. Many of our fellow-men have, since its commencement, passed into eternity, their season of grace fled for ever. We are still spared. The living monuments of thy grace, we shall praise thee, as we do together this night.

We bless thee especially for the tokens of thy mercy in Jesus. We bless thee for his full, free, everlasting redemption. Let us feel the all-sufficiency and security of his covenant love. That for infinite want there is infinite fulness,—that for infinite danger there is an infinite salvation.

Lord, give us grace to live worthy of our high calling. Enable us to adorn the doctrine of our God and Savior. Let his love be the animating principle in our actions. Let our chief delight be to serve him—our greatest pain to vex and grieve him. May our affections be more elevated— our eye more single—our lives more consistent—religion more the one thing needful. Enable us to exercise a child-like submission in thy dealings. These may at times be mysterious; but when thy purposes of love are at last unfolded, we shall dwell with adoring gratitude on all the way by which thou hast led us. Give us grace, meanwhile, to be living as dying creatures.

Look in kindness on this household; may they all have the rich and enduring heritage of those that fear thy name. Bless all our absent friends. Be thou ever present with them. If there be any still at a distance from thee, Lord, bring them nigh, through the blood of the everlasting covenant. Let not one be found wanting at the Great Day.

We pray for thy Church universal. O thou Great High Priest, do thou feed every golden candlestick with the oil of thy grace. Be thou the "all in all" of every church, as of every believer. Do thou promote union among thy true people. Let them not live apart, looking coldly and distantly on one another. Feeling that they are all one in Christ Jesus, may they love one another with a pure heart fervently; and thus the Church on earth may be a dim reflection of the glorious Church of thy redeemed in heaven.

Hear us in these prayers, O our Father, and let our lives hereafter, if we should be spared to see the light of another day, correspond with the expressions of our prayers, that we may live by faith in the Word of God, and die in that faith, and enter into the joy of our Lord.

Watch over us during the silence and darkness of another night; and spare us, if it be thy will, to see the light, and to enjoy the comforts of another day.

Hear these our humble supplications. And all that we ask is for Jesus' sake. Amen.

SATURDAY MORNING.

AND if children, then heirs; heirs of God, and joint-heirs with Christ.—Rom. viii. 17.

For which cause He is not ashamed to call them brethren.—Heb· ii. 11.

Almighty God, our Heavenly Father. We thank thee that we are again permitted to draw near to a throne of grace to worship thee. Thou hast watched over us during the night and brought us to see the light of another day.

Anew we draw near to the opened fountain ;—anew, gracious Savior, we plead thy spotless merits. It was thine own errand of wondrous love,—that which brought thee from thy throne in heaven,—to proclaim liberty to the captives, and the opening of the prison to them that are bound. Do thou usher us into the glorious liberty of thy people. May we feel that there is no real happiness indesendent of thee ;—that all else are walking in a vain show— seeking rest but finding none. But if thou make us free, we shall be free indeed. Enable us to take thee as the strength of our hearts and our portion for ever.

Keep us from the absorbing power of earthly things. Let us not be dead to thee, and alive only to a dead and dying world. Let not the seen and the temporal eclipse the higher and nobler objects of faith. May we live under the powers of a world to come,—loving thee now with some feeble and imperfect foretaste of that love with which we trust we shall love thee for ever.

We rejoice to believe that we are entirely in thy keeping. If thou sendest us prosperity, Lord, hallow it. If thou sendest us adversity, Lord, sanctify it. May all things work together for our good and thy glory.

We commend to thy gracious providence those in whom we are more specially interested. Take our friends under thy peculiar care. Sanctify them by the indwelling of thy Holy Spirit ;—prosper them outwardly and inwardly ;—may all their duties and occupations be leavened with godliness. Bless our own immediate circle :—may God be our Father, and Jesus our elder Brother, and heaven our everlasting home. Bless the young—defend them from this present evil world. Let them early know the happiness of seeking and finding the one thing needful.

May thy kingdom come. Support and strengthen all devoted laborers in heathen lands. May thy Spirit come down as rain upon the mown grass—as showers that water the earth. Sanctify affliction to all in sorrow. Let thy suffering people rejoice in the assurance that thy chastisements are the dealings of a Father ; that the furnace is lighted to purge away the dross, and refine and purify for glory.

Direct, control, suggest, this day, all our thoughts, purposes, designs, and actions, that we may consecrate soul and body, with all their powers, to the glory of thy holy name. And all that we ask or hope for, is for the Redeemer's sake. Amen.

SATURDAY EVENING.

AND they shall be mine, saith the Lord of hosts, in that day when I make up my jewels; and I will spare them, as a man spareth his own son that serveth him.—Mal. iii. 17.

O Lord, we desire to approach thy throne of grace this evening, adoring thee as God over all, blessed for evermore. Draw near to us as we draw near to thee. We bless thee that thou hast spared us during another day, and another week. Let us end every day and every week as if these might possibly be our last; as if the midnight cry might break upon our ears ere we see another rising sun, or a returning Sabbath.

We come, acknowledging, that it is of the Lord's mercies that we are not consumed. By nature and by wicked works we could *expect* nothing, but indignation and wrath, tribulation and anguish. Each day is a witness against us. We confess our proneness to depart from thee the living God,—our reluctance to render to thee the tribute of our undivided homage and love.

Lord, we bring our sins and lay them on him, who was wounded for our transgressions, and bruised for our iniquities. We bring our weakness to his almighty strength; we bring our insufficiency, that we may receive from him, the promised " all-sufficiency in all things." We rejoice, blessed Savior, to think of thee, as sympathizing with us in all our trials and perplexities and temptations;— keeping us as the apple of thine eye, and feeling what is done to thy people as if it were done to thyself. Enable us to repose in the infinite fullness of thy grace and mercy; to experience the blessedness of an unreserved, unwavering trust and confidence in thy dealings. Let us confide to thee the allotment of all that befalls us. Let us harbor no suspicions of thy faithfulness and love. Let us commit the unknown future to thy better wisdom, saying, "Teach us the way wherein we shall walk, for we lift our souls unto thee."

O God, while we pray for ourselves we would remember before thee all whom we ought to remember at a throne of grace. Prosper thy cause and kingdom in the world. Bring the wickedness of the wicked to an end; may the Prince of Peace take to himself his great power and reign. Bless the young; may they spring up as willows by the water-courses: may they be trees of righteousness, the planting of the Lord. Bless the aged; may they be gathered into the garner of the great husbandman, as a shock of corn in its season; full of years and ripe for glory.

Bless all thy faithful ministers—especially those who, to-morrow, are to proclaim thy holy word;—strengthen them outwardly and inwardly, as they go forth, bearing the precious seed; and on the great reaping-day of judgment, may they come again with rejoicing, bringing their sheaves with them. Bless us as a family. Let us all own one common Master—one Father in heaven.

Be with us throughout the silent watches of the night. Whether we wake or sleep, may we live together with thee. There is no darkness to us if thou art with us. Defend us during the unconscious hours of slumber, that we may rise on thy holy Sabbath fitted for duty, happy in the assured continuance of thy favor and love. And all we ask is for Jesus Christ's sake. Amen.

SUNDAY MORNING.

WHEN the fulness of the time was come, God sent forth his Son, made of a woman, made under the law, to redeem them that were under the law, that we might receive the adoption of sons.— Gal. iv. 4, 5.

Almighty and everlasting God, we bless thee for the return of another day of the Son of man. We thank thee that we have been spared during another week, while many of our fellow-men have been called to render in their account. Give us filial nearness to thee our Father in heaven. Let us hear thy gracious benediction—" Peace be unto you." May thine own day be begun, carried on, and ended, under a sense of thy presence and favor. May all worldly thoughts, and cares, and disquietudes, be laid aside, that we may enjoy a fortaste of the everlasting blessedness which is at thy right hand.

We come, gracious Lord, relying on thy mercy and love in Jesus. We would direct the undivided eye of faith to his finished salvation ; rejoicing that it is as free as ever, and as efficacious as ever. Fill us with a deep and humbling sense of our sins. May we mourn an erring past, and receive grace for an unknown future. We would seek this day anew to enkindle our love at thy holy altar. Inspire us with resolutions of new obedience. May we no longer live unto ourselves—to the world—to the creature —to sin. May the great Creator and the adorable Redeemer occupy, without a rival, the throne of our affections. Let us cultivate a holy fear of offending thee. May the love of God be shed abroad in our hearts, by the Holy Ghost, given unto us.

We desire to remember. in thy presence, all in whom we are interested. Bless thy people, this day, throughout the Christian world; may multitudes be added to the Church, of such as shall be saved. Strengthen thy ministering servants in the proclamation of thy holy word. May many careless souls be arrested; may weak ones be strengthened; may sorrowing ones be comforted; may the weary and heavy-laden obtain rest. May a Sabbath-spirit follow us all throughout the week; and may this day—the memorial of the Savior's resurrection—be to us also an earnest of the everlasting rest which remains for thy people in glory.

We commend our dear friends especially to thy protection. May they, too, be in the Spirit on the Lord's day; may they call and find the Sabbath a delight. Keep them, good Lord, by thy mighty power. May they live soberly, and righteously, and godly, in this present world; looking for that blessed hope, even the glorious appearing of the great God our Savior. Bless the members of our family circle; keep them ever near to thee.

Sanctify trial to the sons and daughters of affliction. May they bow in submission to thy sovereign appointments, saying, "Even so, Father! for so it seems good in thy sight."

Lord, take the charge of us; and when thy will concerning us on earth is completed, take us to dwell with thyself in glory everlasting; and all we ask is for the Redeemer's sake. Amen.

SUNDAY EVENING.

HAVE we not all one Father? hath not one God created us?—Mal. ii. 10.

Thou, O Lord, art our Father, our Redeemer; Thy name is from everlasting.—Isa. lxiii. 16.

O God our heavenly Father, who hearest prayer, unto thee we come. Thou never hast said unto anyone, Seek ye my face in vain. Thy thoughts to us are unchanging thoughts of love.

We approach thee on this the evening of thy holy Day, acknowledging our great unworthiness. Fill us with a deep sense of our sins. We are apt to plead vain excuses, if not to thee, yet to ourselves, for our sins.

Forgive us, O Lord,—forgive us all, for thy dear Son's sake. Wash these crimson and scarlet stains away, in the fountain opened for sin and for uncleanness. Let us know more and more the preciousness of the faithful saying, that " Jesus Christ came into the world to save sinners."

Enable us to live as thy redeemed children. As he who hath called us is holy, so may we be holy in all manner of conversation. Put thy fear in our hearts;—not the fear of torment, but the child-like fear of offending so kind a Father—so gracious and forgiving a Savior. Blessed Lord, make these unworthy hearts of ours thy temple;— holy altars of gratitude and love. May our lives form a continued thank-offering for thy manifold mercies. May we count it our highest privilege, as well as our sacred duty, to walk so as to please thee. Let us be growing in faith and love—in charity and meekness—rejoicing in hope of the glory of God.

Father, glorify thy name. Darkness is still covering the lands, and gross darkness the people. May the time to favor Zion, yea, the set time, speedily come. Revive thy work in the midst of the years;—in wrath do thou remember mercy.

We pray for all in affliction. O thou who art the healer of the broken-hearted, the comforter of all that are cast down—do thou impart to every sorrowing, bereaved spirit, thine own everlasting consolations. May all thy suffering people come forth as gold tried in the fire; and so be found at last unto praise and honor and glory at the appearing of Jesus Christ.

We commend our family and household to thy care. God of Bethel, God of our fathers, the God and Father of our Lord Jesus Christ, be thou the covenant God of all near and dear to us. Whether they be now present or absent, may they all be near and dear to thee. Keeper of Israel, be thou their Keeper; guide them, guard them, sanctify them; use them for thy service here, and bring them to the enjoyment of thyself hereafter.

Take us under thy providential care this night. When the gates of the morning are again opened, may it be to hear thy benediction and blessing—" Fear not, for I am with thee." And all that we ask is for the sake of him whom thou hearest always; and to whom, with thee, the Father, and thee, O blesseed Spirit, one God, be everlasting praise, honor, and glory, world without end. Amen.

MONDAY MORNING.

H E shall cry unto me, Thou art my father, my God, and the rock
of my salvation.—Ps. lxxxix. 26.

Almighty God, we desire, on this, the morning of a
new day, to approach thy throne of grace. Thou art glorious in thy holiness, fearful in praises, continually doing
wonders. Thine eternity no finite mind can fathom : thy
purposes no accident can alter : thy love no time can im-
pair. We adore thee as the God of our life ; moment by
moment we are dependent on thy goodness ; if thou with-
drawest thy hand, we perish.

And yet, O Lord, we have not been living habitually
mindful of thee. We have too often taken our blessings as
matters of course. We have had unthankful spirits in the
midst of daily tokens of unmerited mercy. Above all, we
have been living in guilty forgetfulness of thy dear Son.
We have not been remembering as we ought, that but for
him and his wondrous grace, we must have perished forever. We have not felt, as we ought, the attractive power
of his cross. We have been " minding earthly things ; "
too often careful, and troubled, and concerned, about what
will perish with the very using.

Lord, have mercy upon us. Melt our hard and ob-
durate hearts ; renew them by the indwelling of thy gracious Spirit. Give us henceforth a more ardent ambition to
serve thee. All our hope is in Jesus. Help us, blessed
Savior, else we die ! There is infinite merit in thee to meet
all the magnitude of infinite guilt. May we exhibit more
willingness to renounce all dependence on ourselves, that

thou mayest be enthroned in our hearts, as Lord of all. Make us more heavenly-minded. Our graces are feeble— Lord, sustain them. Our affections are lukewarm—Lord, revive them. Search us—try us—lead us; use what discipline thou seest best: may it all result in our growing sanctification,—in endearing to us thy favor, and bringing us to live under a more constant and realizing sense of the things which cannot be shaken, but remain.

We pray for a world lying in wickedness. How long shall the wicked—how long shall the wicked triumph? Save thy people, and bless thine inheritance, feed them also, and lift them up for ever. Bless abundantly the preaching of thy holy word. Glorify thyself in the salvation of sinners. May the hands of thy ministering servants be made strong by the arms of the mighty God of Jacob; may bows, this day, drawn at a venture, have carried the arrow of conviction or of comfort to many hearts.

We commend to thee all who are near and dear to us. May they be shielded by thy providence, and sanctified by thy grace. May they feel that to be spiritually-minded is life and peace. Bless our own family,—preserve us by thy mighty power. May we all feel that it is thou, Lord, only, who makest us to dwell in safety.

We put ourselves, this day, and ever, at thy disposal. May the everlasting arms be around us for good;—guiding through life—through death—till we are safe in glory;— through Jesus Christ, our only Lord and Savior. Amen.

MONDAY EVENING.

B^E ye followers [imitators] of God, as dear children: and walk in, love, as Christ also hath loved us.—Eph. v. 1, 2.

O Lord, our Heavenly Father, by whose good providence we are spared from day to day, do thou enable us to come this night into thy presence, with hearts filled with gratitude and thankfulness for all thy mercies. We would be deeply humbled on account of our unworthiness. What are we, that we should be permitted to take thy name into our lips? We have sinned, what shall we say unto thee, O thou preserver and Redeemer of men? We have erred and strayed from thy ways like lost sheep; we have followed too much the devices and the desires of our own hearts unto evil. We have been living in the enjoyment of countless blessings without any due acknowledgment of thy giving hand. Thy kindness has too often been abused, thy grace resisted. We have been worshiping and serving the creature more than the Creator, who is God over all, blessed for evermore.

What encouragement we have to trust thy love and mercy! We can fear no evil when thou art with us. We rejoice that we are in thy hands;—that all that concerns us and ours is at thy disposal. Enable us to rest, in calm composure, in thine infinite wisdom. Give us lowliness and gentleness; kindness and unselfishness. May our own wills be merged in the higher will of our Father in heaven. Whatever be the discipline thou employest, may we meekly submit to it. May we watch all thy varied teachings, and

get profit and sanctification out of them all. May they
bring us nearer to heaven and nearer to thee.

Lord, we flee anew to the clefts of the Smitten Rock;
—hide us there, from that wrath and everlasting condemnation which these our manifold sins have justly merited.

Bless our household;—unite us, as a family, in the
bonds of peace. May the blood of the everlasting covenant be sprinkled on the portals of every heart. We pray
for our native land. Bless our rulers, and judges, and sen-
ators; may they be a terror to evil-doers, and a praise to
them that do well. Bless the ministers of the everlasting
Gospel; may they be workmen needing not to be ashamed,
rightly dividing the word of truth. Whatever, O God, our
station in life may be, may we seek to do something for the
glory of thy holy name. Give us grace to work while it is
called to-day. May our loins be girded and our lights
burning; may we be like those who are waiting for their
Lord, that when he cometh and knocketh, we may be ready
to open to him immediately. Watch over us during this
night. Grant us refreshing rest;—and spare us, if it be thy
will, to see the light of a new day. And all that we ask is
for the sake of him whom thou hearest always, and to
whom, with thee, the Father, and thee, ever blessed Spirit,
one God, be ascribed everlasting praise, honor, and glory,
world without end. Amen.

TUESDAY MORNING.

AS many as received him, to them gave he power to become the sons of God, even to them that believe on his name.—Jno. i. 12.

O Lord, we desire to draw near into thy blessed presence on this the beginning of a new day. Do thou accept of our morning sacrifice. Throughout the day may our minds be stayed on thee. May a sense of thy favor and love be intermingled with all its duties, hallowing all its pleasures, and softening all its trials. Lord, we have received our being from thy hands;—may the lives imparted by thee, and sustained by thee, be consecrated to thy praise. May we feel the happiness of thy service, and regard nothing that this world can give, as comparable to the enjoyment of thy friendship and love.

We thank thee, above all, for the provisions of the everlasting covenant. Gracious Savior—thou Shepherd—Guide—and Portion of thy people, give us the assured sense of pardon and forgiveness through the blood of the Cross. May simple faith be followed by holy obedience, May we know the blessedness of a holy life; of affections once alienated from God, now alienated from the world. May no spiritual foe be permitted to obtain the victory over us; no idol to usurp thy place in our souls. May we have strength given us either to perform or to endure thy will, and to cleave unto thee with full purpose of heart.

We pray for all mankind; visit, in mercy, the dark places of the earth, which are still the habitations of cruely. Strengthen thy missionary servants. Arouse thy churches to greater zeal in the promotion of thy cause. We would pray the Lord of the harvest that he would send forth laborers to his harvest.

God of our fathers, be our covenant God. Dwell in this family and household : hallow every heart as an altar to thy praise. Impress upon us all a family resemblance to the Great Elder Brother, our living Head in glory. Each of us is advancing nearer eternity ; may we seek to be becoming more and more meet for our everlasting home. Prepare us for the blessedness of uninterrupted fellowship with thyself hereafter.

Have compassion on all who are afflicted. Pity the houseless poor, the orphaned children, the widowed heart. O thou, who turnest the shadow of death into the morning —do thou console and comfort them. May they adore thee, alike in giving and in taking away ;—in the bestowing of thy gifts, and in the removing them ; saying, in devout submission, " Blessed be the name of the Lord."

We commit ourselves to thy care. May the Lord God this day be to us a sun and shield. May the Lord give grace and glory, and withhold from us nothing that he sees to be truly good. And all that we ask is for Jesus' sake. Amen.

TUESDAY EVENING.

BLESSED are the peacemakers: for they shall be called the children of God.—Matt. v. 9.

O Lord our God, we thank thee that we are again permitted, in the multitude of thy mercies, to see the close of another day. We desire to end it with thee. Ere we retire to rest, we would implore thee for thy blessing and guardian care. Make not our pillow this night a pillow of death. Give thine angels charge over us during the unconscious hours of sleep; and when we awake, may we be still with thee.

We adore thee, gracious God, as the source of all our happiness—the Author of all our blessings. We desire to take thee as our chief joy. Guide us by thy counsel. Thou hast been gracious to us in the past; we will trust thee in the future. Let our heartfelt wish and longing be —to live, and walk, and act, so as to please thee: and thus may each returning night, as it finds us nearer eternity, find us better prepared for the enjoyment of thy presence for ever.

Cleanse us from all the defilements of the day; all our sins of omission and commission. Accept of us in the Beloved. Adored be thy name, we have in Jesus the Physician who healeth all our diseases. We stand now, as we desire to stand on the Judgment-day, clothed in his spotless righteousness.

We commend, holy Father, to thy gracious care and providence, our family and household. May each of us be a member of the household of faith. Do thou, if it be thy will, long continue unbroken our home-circle on earth ; but let our true home be in heaven. Let the watchword of each, near and dear to us, be this—" We are journeying unto the place of which the Lord hath said, I will give it you." Bless the young ; train them early for glory. Preserve them from the countless temptations of a world lying in wickedness. We pray for the afflicted ; we commend them to him who knows their frame.

Let thy kingdom come. Stand by thy missionary servants; may they have many heathen souls for their hire ; many, who shall be to them as a crown of joy and rejoicing on the Great Day.

Known unto thee are all our wants ; we leave our petitions at the footstood of thy throne, assured that in thee we have a rich Provider. And when the provisions of the earthly journey are needed no more, may it be our blessed privilege to feed on the Bread which endureth to everlasting life. And all that we ask is in the name and for the sake of him whom thou hearest always ; and to whom, with thee the Father, and thee, O Eternal Spirit, one God, be ascribed all blessing, and honor, and glory, and praise, world without end. Amen.

WEDNESDAY MORNING.

A ND because ye are sons, God hath sent forth the Spirit of his Son
into your hearts, crying, Abba, Father.—Gal. iv. 6.

O Lord, thou art great, and greatly to be feared, thy
greatness is unsearchable. Who shall not fear thee, and
glorify thy name? for thou only art holy. Eternal Father,
who hast loved us with an everlasting love:—Eternal Son,
who did so freely shed thy precious blood for us:—Eternal
Spirit, who art waiting and willing to renew and sanctify—
yea, to make these worthless souls of ours temples to thy
praise;—Do thou come to us in the plenitude of thy love
this morning, that we may feel it to be good for us to draw
near unto God.

What are our lives, but testimonies to divine faithfulness? We look back with gratitude and thankfulness on a
wondrous past,—the mercies innumerable which have been
showered upon us, and that, too, in the midst of ingratitude
and sin. Bless the Lord, O our souls, and forget not all
his benefits!

Where could we now have been, but for thy great love
to us in Christ! On him our every hope of pardon and
acceptance is built. On his work we desire every hour to
live. We rejoice that we have such a Day's-Man between
us, who has laid his hand upon us both; that he is now
pleading for us within the veil—answering for those who
cannot answer for themselves. Lord, enable us to manifest
our love to him, by a holy walk and conversation, adorning
the doctrine of God our Savior in all things. Give us a

tender conscience, a broken spirit, filial nearness, purity of heart, consistency of conduct, uprightness of life. Loving thee, our God, may we love also our fellow-men. Bring us under the power of renewed natures and purified affections. May all that is earthly and carnal, all that is unamiable and selfish, all that is unkind and unholy, be displaced by what is pure, elevated, lovely, and of good report. Above all, may we live under the influence of unseen realities. Stablish our hearts with the blessed truth, that the coming of the Lord draweth nigh; that so, when the hour of death shall overtake us, it may be to us an angel whispering, "The Master is come, and calleth for thee."

Bless us as a family;—give us the heritage of those that fear thy name; may the absent know thee as ever present;—and when earth's separations are at an end, may there be a common meeting-place for us all at last, before thy throne.

Be our God and guide this day; protect our bodies from danger, preserve our souls from sin; never leave and never forsake us. And all that we ask is in the name, and for the sake of Jesus Christ, our blessed Lord and Savior. Amen.

WEDNESDAY EVENING.

A S many as are led by the Spirit of God, they are the sons of God
  . . . The Spirit itself beareth witness with our spirit, that we
are the children of God.—Rom. viii. 14, 16.

Most blessed God, we desire to approach thy sacred
presence on this the close of another day. Let our prayer
come before thee as incense, and the lifting up of our hands
as the evening sacrifice. Glory be to thy holy name, that
though heaven is thy dwelling place, thou condescendest
also to make every lowly heart thy habitation. Though
thou art the greatest of all beings, thou art the kindest of
all, and the best of all.

We come, weak and helpless and burdened, to that
cross where alone there is shelter and peace for the guilty.
We will not cloak nor dissemble our manifold sins and
wickedness before the face of thee, our Heavenly Father.
We would confess them with an humble, lowly, penitent,
and obedient heart.

Blessed Jesus, we rejoice to think of thee as thou now
art, the unchanging Intercessor within the Veil, with all
the might of infinite Godhead, and all the tenderness and
pity of compassionate man. May we cleave to thee now,
and serve thee now, that we may not be ashamed before
thee at thy coming. Let it be our endeavor to show that
we are Christians indeed,—living Epistles, known and read
of all men. Let us be gentle, and kind, and forgiving.
Let us not be betrayed into anger or uncharitableness.
Let patience have its perfect work. May we be willing to

do all, and to *bear* all, for the sake of him who hath done so much and borne so much for us. Give us a solemn sense of responsibility for every talent committed to our keeping. Let us feel that they are not given merely to be enjoyed by *us*, but to be employed for *thee*. Alive to our stewardship, may we lay them out for thy glory and for our own and our neighbors' good.

Bless all our beloved friends; remember them with thy special favor :—wherever they are, may they know the true blessedness of life, when spent in thy service. We pray for all poor afflicted ones. Ease their burdens— soothe their sorrows—dry their tears—enable them meekly to repose in thy covenant faithfulness and love.

And now, Lord, what wait we for? our hope is in thee. Most graciously answer us, not according to our own wishes, but according to what thou knowest would be best. We are poor and needy, yet the Lord thinketh upon us.

Guard us through the night. Give thine angels charge concerning us, that they may encamp round about us. Whether we wake or sleep, may we live together with thee. And all that we ask is for the sake of him whom thou hearest always, and to whom, with thee and the Holy Ghost we will ascribe all glory and honor, now and forever. Amen.

THURSDAY MORNING.

VERILY, verily, I say unto you, Whatsoever ye shall ask the Father
in my name, he will give it you.—John xvi. 23.

Almighty Father, thou art from everlasting to everlasting God. We adore thee as the Author of our existence, and the source of all our happiness. We desire to
connect every blessing we possess with thee, the great
Fountain-head. Thou alone, amid all changes, art the unchanging One. Heaven and earth shall pass away, but
thou are the same, and thy years shall not fail.

We come, poor and needy, pleading thine own gracious promise to give "all sufficiency in all things" to those
who seek thee. We have no offering of our own to present
at thy footstool;—we have everything to receive. There is
nothing between us and everlasting destruction, but thy
mercy in Jesus.

Blessed Savior, do thou say unto each of us, " Your
sins are forgiven you." Bring us to live, more and more
every day, under the constraining influence of thy love.
Being made free from sin, and having become thy covenant
servants, may we have our fruit unto holiness. May we be
gaining fresh victories over our secret corruptions. May
the power of evil wax weaker and weaker; and the power
of thy grace wax stronger and stronger. May we know,
by joyful experience, the happiness of true holiness.

Give us reverential and child-like submission to thy
will. Finite wisdom has no place in thy dealings : not
only are all things ordained by thee, but ordained in ineffa-

ble wisdom and love. May the end of thy dispensations be our growing sanctification.

Mercifully accommodate the supplies of thy grace to the sons and daughters of sorrow. May they call upon thee in the day of trouble, and do thou deliver them ; and though it may not be the deliverance they would have de-'sired, may it lead them to " glorify thee."

Look in kindness on our family circle ; may thy name be ever hallowed here; may we know the happiness of that household whose God is the Lord. Bless our beloved friends who may be absent from us. If separated from one another now, may we meet at last in the better country, and together enter into the joy of our Lord. Be thou with us throughout this day. May thy peace be upon us and upon all the Israel of God. Guide us by thy counsel ; strengthen us for duty; and prepare us for trial. In all our ways we would acknowledge thee, and do thou direct our paths. And all we ask is for the Redeemer's sake. Amen.

THURSDAY EVENING.

FOR the earnest expectation of the creature waiteth for the manifes-
tation of the sons of God . . . Because the creature itself also
shall be delivered from the bondage of corruption into the glorious
liberty of the children of God.—Romans viii. 19, 21.

O God, thou art great and greatly to be feared, thy
greatness is unsearchable. Heaven is thy throne,—the
earth is thy footstool. Before thee, cherubim and seraphim
continually do cry—Holy, holy, holy, is the Lord God of
Hosts: heaven and earth are full of the majesty of thy
glory. Thou art the sovereign controller of all events.
Thou doest according to thy will in the armies of heaven
and among the inhabitants of the earth. The Lord reigneth. Man proposeth, but God disposeth ; and he disposeth
wisely and well.

We bless thee, that as sinners we are permitted to
come, with all the load of our guilt, to a great Savior. We
will arise and go to our Father ; we will say, Father, we
have sinned against heaven and in thy sight,—we are no
more worthy to be called thy children ! But do thou for
Jesus' sake, thine own dear Son, have mercy upon us miserable offenders. Behold, O God, our shield : look upon
us in the face of thine Anointed. Wash us in his blood ;
clothe us with his righteousness : sanctify us by the indwelling of thy Holy Spirit, and present us at last, faultless before the presence of thy glory with exceeding joy.

May the life of Jesus be made manifest in our mortal
flesh. May our citizenship be more in heaven ; may we
bear upon us the lofty impress of those who are born *from*

above, and *for* above,—and who declare plainly that they seek a better country.

Whatever be the sphere in which thy good providence has placed us, may it be our earnest endeavor to use our time, and talents, and opportunities for thee. Our season of probation must soon be finished : may we work while it is called to-day, remembering that the night cometh.

Look in kindness on thy church universal. Revive thy work in the midst of the years. Return, O Lord, and visit this vineyard which thine own right hand hath planted; may every branch be laden with fruit ; found unto praise, and honor, and glory, at the appearing of Jesus Christ.

Compassionate the afflicted : comfort all who are cast down. Be the helper of the helpless ; the refuge of the distressed; the father of the fatherless. May all mourning the loss of beloved friends be led to bow submissively to thy sovereign will, and look forward with joyful hearts to that better time and that better world, where the fountain of these tears shall be for ever dried.

Give us all the heritage of thy grace and love, and then we shall be rich indeed. Many are saying, " Who will show us any good ? " May *we* have but one wish, " Lift thou, upon us and ours, the light of thy countenance." Be with us this night. It is thou, Lord, only who makest us to dwell in safety. When we lie down to rest, let the curtain of thy protecting providence be drawn around us, and when we awake may we still be with thee. And all that we ask is in the name and for the sake of the Lord Jesus, to whom, with thee and the Holy Spirit, be all honor and glory, world without end. Amen.

FRIDAY MORNING.

FEAR not little flock; for it is your Father's good pleasure to give you the kingdom.—Luke xii. 32.

O God, our heavenly Father, we desire, on this the morning of a new day, to bow before thy throne of grace. We thank thee for thy guardianship and care during the unconscious hours of sleep. Thou hast dispersed the darkness of another night, and permitted the sun once more to arise upon us. O thou better Sun of Righteousness, do thou disperse the deeper darkness of sin ; shine on us with the brightness of thy rising; let us enjoy this day the blessedness of peace with God.

Lord Jesus, we commit our temporal and eternal interests anew to thy keeping. Soul and body are thine by thy redemption purchase. May they become temples of the Holy Ghost, with this as their superscription, " Holiness to the Lord." May nothing that is unclean or that defileth enter therein. May it be our sovereign motive, to walk so as to please thee. May it be our heaviest cross and trial, to incur thy displeasure. Let us not be content with a mere name to live. Give us grace, that we may be enabled to do thy will and promote thy glory. In the performance of every-day duty, let us seek to make this the directory of our conduct—" How would Jesus have acted here ? " May we put on, as the elect of God, holy and beloved, bowels of mercies, kindness, humbleness of mind, meekness, long-suffering, forbearing one another, and forgiving one another, if any have a quarrel against any, even as Christ hath forgiven us, so may we do also.

We pray for all in sorrow. O thou God of all consolation, be a Father to the fatherless, a Husband to the widow, the stranger's shield, and the orphan's stay. Enable thy suffering people to rest in thy love—saying, The Lord's will be done.

Bless our beloved friends ; if there.be any among them who are still strangers to thee, Lord, reveal to them thy dear Son in all his ability to save. Preserve us as a household from danger and sin ; keep us in the hollow of thy hand ; and may death, when it comes, be to all of us the entrance to glory. May thy Church universal live in the unity of the Spirit, and in the bond of peace. Revive thy work in the midst of the years ; may the day soon arrive, when all ends of the earth shall see the salvation of God.

Listen, gracious Father, to these our supplications ; when thou hearest, forgive ; and grant us an answer in peace, for the Redeemer's sake. Amen.

FRIDAY EVENING.

A ND he said unto him, Son, thou art ever with me, and all that I
have is thine.—Luke xv. 31.

Gracious Father, we approach thy throne this evening,
adoring thee as the God of our life and the length of our
days. We bless thee for the many tokens of thy love daily
bestowed upon us : for food and raiment—for health and
strength—for friends and home—for all that brightens our
pathway in life—for all that cheers and brightens our pros-
pects beyond the grave. Lord, how often hast thou disappointed our fears, answered our prayers, and fulfilled our
hopes ; how often has thy grace made arduous duties easy,
and levelled mountains of difficulty ! How often, when our
hearts were overwhelmed, hast thou led us to the Rock that
is higher than we ; and given us help from trouble, when
vain was the help of man !

We come anew to thee this night, weary and heavy-
laden, beseeching thee to grant us the blessed sense of thy
forgiving mercy. We lament that we do not feel, as we
ought, the burden of sin. Show us the infinite adaptation
of the Redeemer, in his person and work, to meet all the
necessities of our tried and tempted natures. May his
name be as ointment poured forth ; may his blood be our
only plea—his love our animating principle—his glory our
chief end. May our souls become holy altars from which
the incense of obedience ascends continually. May we be
enabled to *do* thy will and to *love* thy will, because it is
thine. May our eye be single that our whole body may be

full of light. Oh keep us from temptation ; support and deliver us when we are tempted. May we be able to say, in reply to all the seductive allurements of the Evil One, "How can I do this great wickedness, and sin against God ?"

Sanctify affliction to all thine afflicted people. Let them know that Thy chastisements are mercies in disguise; that Thou watchest every sheep in the fold; and when led out to the rougher parts of the wilderness, Thou " goest before them."

We pray for those who are living without God, and therefore without hope. Let them not put off until it be too late; until they are forced, with unavailing tears, to mourn wasted hours and forfeited opportunities. Convince every procrastinater that now is the accepted time,—that now is the day of salvation.

Bless us, even us, O God, who are now bending at Thy mercy-seat ; rebuke our faithlessness—warm our love— quicken our graces :—let us live more constantly under the powers of a world to come. Ere we lie down on our nightly pillows, we would lay our sins afresh on the head of the Great Surety, that so we may retire to rest at peace with Thee ; and if Thou seest meet to spare us till to-morrow, may we rise fitted for all its duties. Hear these our humble supplications; when Thou hearest, forgive ; and all that we ask is for the Redeemer's sake. Amen.

SATURDAY MORNING.

BUT now, O Lord, thou art our father; we are the clay, and thou our potter; and we all are the work of thy hand.—Isa. lxiv. 8.

Thou, O Lord, art our father, our redeemer; thy name is from everlasting.—Isa. lxiii. 16.

Most blessed God, who art making the outgoings of the evening and the morning to rejoice over us—we desire to begin this new day with Thee. We bless Thee for Thy sparing mercy; in having permitted us once more to lie down to sleep, and to awake in safety and comfort; may we be enabled, as dependents on thy bounty, to receive every returning morning as a fresh pledge of thy love.

We confess, O God, our unworthiness; the alienation of our hearts from thyself, the source of all life and joy and blessedness. But we bless thee, that where sin abounded, grace hath much more abounded. Thanks be unto God for his unspeakable gift; for all that Jesus died to purchase, and which he is now exalted to bestow.

O thou Lamb of God—thou spotless, sinless Victim— we rely on thy most precious Sacrifice. Lord, may our daily walk be more circumspect and holy. Let us follow thy will whatever it may be—though, at times, it may be at variance with our own,—feeling that the Judge of all the earth must do right, and cannot do wrong. In the spirit of Jesus may we have grace to say—" Even so, Father, for so it seems good in thy sight." Above all, preserve us from the temptations of a world lying in wickedness. May we seek to walk circumspectly: remembering that our time is

short; that we have much to do, and a brief time for doing it.

We entreat thee to look down in special mercy on our
household. Visit us all with the love which thou bearest
to thine own. May the young be guided through the slip-
pery paths of youth ; may they be enabled early to range
themselves on the Lord's side—early to seek thee, that they
may early find thee. Bless those that are absent from us ;
—may they be shielded by thy good providence ;—make
them all the children of God, by faith in Christ Jesus.

Good Lord, be with us during this day ; grant us that
blessing which maketh rich and addeth no sorrow with
it; and when all our days are ended, do thou receive us
into everlasting habitations, for the sake of Jesus Christ, our
only Lord and Savior ; to whom with thee the Father, and
thee ever blessed Spirit, be ascribed all blessing and honor
and glory and praise, world without end. Amen.

SATURDAY EVENING.

WHOM the Lord loveth he correcteth, even as a father the son in
whom he delighteth.—Prov. iii. 12.

O Lord, we approach thy sacred presence, on this the
close of another day, and the end of another week, adoring
thee for thy great goodness. We desire, with united hearts,
to set up our Ebenezer of thankfulness, and to say, " Hitherto hath the Lord helped us." We are utterly unworthy
of the least of all thy mercies. If thou hadst dealt with us
as we deserve, or rewarded us according to our iniquities,
we could not answer for one of a thousand. Through the
doing and·dying of Jesus, the law has been disarmed of its
condemning power; all its penalties have been borne; death
itself has been stript of its terrors, and the Kingdom of
Heaven opened to all believers.

Lord, after such a pledge of thy love, in not sparing
thine own Son, we believe thou wilt with him also freely
give us all things. If thou sendest us prosperity, may we
be enabled to give thee the return of grateful hearts, and
obedient, submissive lives. If thou deny us earthly bliss
and earthly happiness, let us accept the denial as the will of
Infinite Goodness. We will put our trust in thee. In thee
we are as secure as everlasting power and wisdon and love
can make us. If there be times when we are led to exclaim—" Verily thou art a God that hidest thyself," we will
look forward with joy to that better world, where mystery
shall give way to perfect knowledge. Lord, make us more
holy; sanctify us through thy truth; keep us watchful;

keep us humble; keep us from unchristian tempers; keep us from all pride, vain glory, and hypocrisy. Let us cultivate an habitual, realizing sense of thy divine presence; and in our worldly work and calling, whatsoever we do, may we do it heartily as to the Lord and not unto men.

We pray for others as well as for ourselves. Draw near in mercy this night to any who may be in sorrow and distress, or who may be mourning the loss of beloved relatives. Do thou sanctify their trials;—may these yield the peaceable fruits of righteousness.

Bless our beloved friends; write their names in the Lamb's book of life. Bless us who are now surrounding thy footstool; do thou spare us long together as an unbroken circle on earth; and when we shall be called to leave behind us this lower valley, may we be conducted into those blessed regions, which eye hath not seen, nor ear heard; where there shall be no more parting; and where we shall stand without fault before thy throne.

We commend ourselves to thy Fatherly protection during the silent watches of the night. Do thou give us undisturbed repose and refreshing sleep;—may we be permitted to lie down in thy fear, and to awake in thy favor, fitted and prepared for the duties and services of thy holy day. And all that we ask is for Jesus' sake. Amen.

SUNDAY MORNING.

GO to my brethren, and say unto them, I ascend unto my Father and your Father; and to my God, and your God.—John xx. 17.

I will not leave you comfortless [orphans]: I will come to you.—John xiv. 18.

We will extol thee, our God, O King, we will bless thy name for ever and ever; every day will we bless thee, and we will praise thy name for ever and ever. We thank thee for the return of another Sabbath. Again hast thou permitted us to awake in safty, and not suffered our eyes to sleep the sleep of death. May it prove a holy day of rest to each of us; a rest from sin and a rest in God. May we welcome with gladness of heart the return of these peaceful hours. May all vain and worldly thoughts be set aside; and may we be enabled to worship thee in the beauty of holiness.

But where withal, Lord, shall we come into thy presence? Our very prayers might be enough to condemn us. Our purest services, if weighed in the balances, might rise up in judgement against us.

We come anew in the name of thy dear Son, confessing, and desiring deeply to feel as we confess, that we are sinners. We look to grace abounding over sin,—to infinite merit abounding over infinite demerit,—the everlasting righteousness and faithfulness of a tried Redeemer, coming in the room of our imperfections. We bless thee that Christ ever liveth and reigneth for our justification. We rejoice to think of him as our Great High Priest, with the names of his covenant people engraven on his heart, bearing them along with him in his every approach to the throne:—that all power in heaven and in earth is intrusted to his hands;—nothing befalls us but by his direction,—nothing is appointed us but what he sees to be for our good.

Lord Jesus, we commit our temporal and our everlasting interests to thy keeping. We rejoice that to thee we can confidently intrust them. Undertake thou for us. Carry on within us thine own work in thine own way. Keep us from all evil that is likely to grieve us. May we know the truth of thine own gracious promise, "As thy day is, so shall thy strength be."

We pray for all in sickness and distress; for those deprived of beloved relatives, and who are mourning those who "are not." May it please thee to bind up their wounds, and to soothe their sorrows: direct the unwavering eye of faith to that better world, where every weight of suffering shall be exchanged for the exceeding weight of glory, and where God shall wipe away all tears from off all faces.

Bless our own family and friends, both present and absent. May the invisible chain of thy covenant-love bind us all together. Strengthen this day the ministers of the everlasting gospel; may great grace be imparted to them; may they come forth fully fraught with the blessings of the gospel of peace: and may all thy churches, walking in the fear of God and in the comfort of the Holy Ghost, everywhere be multiplied. Promote unity and concord among thy true people. May that predicted period soon arrive, when Ephraim shall not vex Judah, nor Judah vex Ephraim; when all shall see eye to eye and heart to heart.

Take us now under thy care, and enable us, whether waking or sleeping, to live together with thee; and all that we ask is for the sake of him whom thou hearest always; to whom with thee and the Holy Ghost be all honor and praise, world without end. Amen.

SUNDAY EVENING.

GIVING thanks always for all things unto God and the Father in the name of our Lord Jesus Christ.—Eph. v. 20.

Most blessed God, whose nature and whose name is love, we desire to draw near into thy gracious presence on this the close of another Sabbath. We thank thee for all the tokens of thy mercy we have been permitted to enjoy. Abide with us, for it is toward evening, and the day is far spent. Under the realizing sense of thy presence and nearness, we would compose ourselves to rest, with our minds stayed on thee.

We desire anew to bless and praise thee for thine unspeakable gift—Jesus the Son of thy love. There is not a ray of hope which visits our souls, but emanates from his cross. He is the channel of every blessing. We rejoice to think that he is as willing as he is able to save "to the uttermost:" that at this moment he is with undying and undiminished love, pleading our cause at the mercy seat.

Do thou follow with thine enriching blessing all the services of the sanctuary. May thy word be quick and powerful:—forbid that impressions be suffered to die away; —do thou fasten them as a nail in a sure place;—and may the Sabbath duties and employments diffuse their solemnity around us throughout the week.

We remember, with affectionate sympathy, the poor, the destitute, and " him that hath no helper;"—the sick— the bereaved—the dying. Lord, draw near to all such; let them know that thou hast grace in store for their every time of need, and that there is no want to them that fear thee. We desire for our friends thy benediction and blessing: the Lord watch between them and us when we are absent one from another: O thou omnipresent God, do thou show that no distance can sever from thee,—give them every token of thy love,—preserve them from danger,—guard them from temptation,—number them with thy saints in glory everlasting. Bless the lambs of the flock—Shepherd of Israel! make them thine;—bringing them to the fold of grace on earth, and to thy heaven of glory hereafter.

Bless that branch of thy chnrch with which we are connected; bless thy holy church universal. Have mercy on those who are still sitting in darkness and in the region and shadow of death. May a lifted-up Savior, by the attractive power of his cross, draw all men unto him.

We commend us, blessed Lord, to thee, and to the word of thy grace. Do thou watch over us during the unconscious hours of sleep. May we awake in the morning in thy favor; that so every new day being spent to thy glory, may find us better fitted for entering on the joys of thine everlasting kingdom; through the merits of Jesus Christ, our only Savior. Amen.

MONDAY MORNING.

B EHOLD, what manner of love the Father hath bestowed upon us,
that we should be called the sons of God.—1 John iii. 1.

O God, thou art the Infinite, Eternal, Unchangeable
Jehovah ; thou art exhalted far above our adorations and
praises : angels and archangels veil their faces with their
wings in thy presence, and cry out, " Unclean, unclean !"

We come, casting ourselves on thy free grace and
mercy in Christ. We rejoice that for the greatest sins
there is a great and all sufficient Savior. There is no load
we have, but he who bore our transgression is able and
willing to remove it. We will rejoice in the Lord, our
souls will be joyful in our God, for he hath clothed us with
the garments of salvation, he hath covered us with a robe
of righteousness.

Thou dost set us in families, and thou dost make men
to be of one mind in a house. Let it be so in this house
to-day ; may we all be of one mind, and live together in
peace, as a Christian household. Make us ready to help
each other, and teach us to be merciful to one another's
faults. Keep us from provoking one another in word or
deed, and make us willing to forgive.

Enable us to walk as it becometh thy children. Give
us a holy fear of offending thee. May we feel all sins to be
grievous in thy sight : but may it be our special desire to
gain fresh victories over our besetting sins, and to be more
and more fortified against the assaults of temptation.
Strengthen us with might by thy Spirit in the inner man.

Make thy grace sufficient for us, and perfect strength [in weakness.

We pray not for ourselves only, but for all whom we ought to remember at a throne of grace. If there be any in whom we are interested who are still far from thee, bring them nigh by the same precious blood. If any are still loitering and lingering, may they hear thy voice, saying,— " Escape for thy life, lest thou be consumed." If there be any backsliding, Lord, reclaim them. If there be any sorrowing, Lord, comfort them. Bind up their broken hearts. Give them thyself—the better portion which never can be taken from them. Thy way is often in the sea, and thy path in the deep waters. But "the Lord reigneth "—may this quiet all doubts. May we wait in patience the great day of disclosures, when "in thy light we shall see light."

Look down in mercy on our family and household; let it be a garden which the Lord hath blessed. May we live in the unity of the Spirit, and in the bond of peace. Keep us this day without sin. Be thou our Shepherd, and we shall not want. Keep us *from*, and keep from *us*, all that would be injurious to our souls' interests ; and, when time shall be no longer, may we meet in the unclouded sunshine of thy presence ; through Jesus Christ, our blessed Lord and Savior. Amen.

MONDAY EVENING.

"YE have not received the spirit of bondage again to fear; but ye have received the Spirit of adoption, whereby we cry, Abba, Father."—Rom. viii. 15.

Most gracious God, Father of all mercies, thou art the King of kings and the Lord of lords;—the Heaven, even the Heaven of heavens, cannot contain thee. Myriads of blessed spirits are continually adoring thee. How shall we, dust and ashes, presume to lift up our eyes to the place where thou in glory dwellest?

To thee, O God, we commit the keeping of our temporal and eternal interests. We cannot be in better hands than in thine. Whether it be to *do*, or to *bear* thy will, may it be ours meekly to say, "Even so, Father!" Whatever may most conduce to thy glory and our good, do thou appoint for us. Be thou ever near us; gladdening us with the continual sense of thy presence and favor. Give us grace ever to realize how short and uncertain our lives are; we cannot tell what a day or an hour may bring forth. Whatsoever our hand findeth to do, may we do it with our might, remembering that there is no device, nor work, nor labor, in the grave whither we are going.

Bless all our dear friends; let them be related to thee in the better bonds of the everlasting covenant; preserve their bodies from danger, and their souls from sin. May our household be a household of faith.

Give us, for our Savior's sake, pardon for all our sins. In his name we beseech thee to take away all our iniquity, to receive us graciously, to love us freely. Let not one un-pardoned sin remain upon us this night.

Bless all who have been kind to us to-day; return their kindness to them sevenfold. Forgive any who have injured us, or spoken against us; forgive and bless them.

Bless those in sorrow. Let this be their comfort in their affliction—"If we suffer with him, we shall be also glorified together:" and let them look forward to that hour, when their sorrow shall be turned into joy; when God himself shall be with them and be their God, and when all tears shall be wiped from off all faces.

Give each of us grace to be so living, that ours at last may be an "abundant entrance" into thine everlasting Kingdom. Keep us waiting—keep us watching; that when the cry shall be heard in the midst of the heavens, "Behold, the Bridegroom cometh," we may be able joy-fully to respond, "Even--so, come, Lord Jesus, come quickly." Ere we lie down to sleep this night, renew to us the gracious sense of sin forgiven; and if spared till to-morrow, let us rise refreshed for duty, and fitted for thy service. And all that we ask, is for the sake of him whom thou hearest always, and to whom with thee, the Father, and thee, O blessed Spirit, one God, be everlasting praise, honor and glory, world without end. Amen.

TUESDAY MORNING.

H E that overcometh shall inherit all things; and I will be his God,
and he shall be my son.—Rev. xxi. 7.

Almighty and everlasting Jehovah, thou art the heart-searching and rein trying God; thou art of purer eyes than to behold iniquity; evil cannot dwell with thee. Thou hast solemnly declared that thou canst by no means clear the guilty. It is only because of thy mercies in Christ, that we are not consumed.

We bless thee for all that Jesus hath done—for all that he is willing to do. We bless thee that he is now exalted a Prince and a Savior; that having purged our sins, he has forever sat down on the right hand of God: and that there he must reign until he hath put all enemies under his feet. Our earnest prayer is, that each of us may be personally and everlastingly interested in his great salvation. May he be precious to us in all his offices, as our Prophet, Priest and King; ruling over us and within us; making our hearts the habitations of God through the Spirit.

Have mercy upon those who are still far from thee. Cause them in their sad and unresting hours of estrangement to think of the Father's heart, the Father's home, the Father's welome. Deepen in them a sense of the misery of alienation, and the happiness of a full and gracious retoration to favor and peace. Confirm the irresolute and wavering in unswerving loyalty and love.

Seeing thou hast loved us with an everlasting love, may we not requite thee with coldness and unthankfulness,

—or give thee the wrecks of "a worn and withered affection." May the best of our thoughts, and the best of our lives, be surrendered to thy service. We would cast all our cares, and every individual care, on thee; knowing and rejoicing that thou "carest for us." Let us trust thee in everything; let us see thy faithfulness in every event in our chequered and changing histories. How thou hast smoothed our way in the past! By thee, our crosses have been lightened; our fears disappointed, our fondest hopes fulfilled. We will trust thee in the future. Let us feel that the great Shepherd, who gave his life for the sheep, cannot lead us wrong.

Bless our dear friends; may the Lord be their keeper; may the sun not smite them by day, nor the moon by night. Do thou preserve them from all evil, in their going out and in their coming in, from this time, henceforth, and even for evermore.

Be thou with us throughout this day; sanctify all its duties; go with us where we go, dwell with us where we dwell: guide us, while we live, by thy counsel, and afterwards receive us into thy glory. Hear us, gracious God, and accept of us for the Redeemer's sake. Amen.

TUESDAY EVENING.

BEHOLD the fowls of the air: for they sow not, neither do they reap, nor gather into barns; yet your heavenly Father feedeth them.—Matt. vi. 26.

Are not two sparrows sold for a farthing? and one of them shall not fall on the ground without your Father. Fear ye not therefore, ye are of more value than many sparrows.—Matt. x. 29, 31.

Heavenly Father, who hast in thy good providence permitted us to meet together this night, be pleased, of thine infinite mercy, to grant us thy blessing. Scatter our darkness with the beams of thy love. Dispel all harassing thoughts, and misgivings, and disquietudes; ere we retire to rest may our souls be stayed on thee. Unto us, O Lord, belong shame and confusion of face. We mourn that we feel so inadequately our guilt and unworthiness. We often confess with the lip what the heart does not feel. We often *appear* to be humble, when we are *not* humble,—when our hearts are full of self, and pride, and vain glory.

We desire to come anew into thy presence, casting ourselves on the free grace, and love, and mercy of Jesus. We rejoice that in his cross all thine attributes have been magnified. Thou art now proclaiming to the vilest and unworthiest, that thou hast no pleasure in the death of the wicked, but rather that he would turn from his wickedness and live. May we be willing to *be* anything, and to *do* anything, and to *suffer* anything for that Savior, who hath done and suffered so much for us; may our only grief be " to give him pain "—may our " joy be to serve and follow him."

We desire to remember before thee all whom we love. Do thou pour thy richest benediction on this our household. Known unto thee are all our varied circumstances, our peculiar trials, and temptations, and perplexities. Our every burden we cast on a faithful God. Our souls, our lives, our cares, we leave entirely in thy hands, saying, "Undertake thou for us."

Pity the afflicted. Be thou the father of the fatherless, the husband of the widow, the stranger's shield, and the orphan's stay; let them know that when heart and flesh faint and fail, thou art the strength of their heart, and their portion forever.

Make us and all our dear friends partakers in the gladness and glory of Christ's resurrection life. May we be one *in* and *with* him now, that so the tenderest ties of earth may be perpetuated before thy throne, and the unstable unions here be there rendered indissoluble.

We now commend us all to thy gracious keeping. The darkness of night has gathered around us; but do thou lift upon us, O God, the light of thy countenance:— it cannot be night if thou art near. Watch over us during sleep, and when we awake may we be still with thee. We ask these, and all other blessings, trusting in the merits and mediation of Jesus Christ, thine only Son, our Savior, who with the Father and the Holy Ghost, ever liveth and reigneth, world without end. Amen.

WEDNESDAY MORNING.

FATHER, I have sinned against heaven, and before thee, and am no more worthy to be called thy son.—Luke xv. 18, 19.

Gracious Father, source and giver of every good and every perfect gift—do thou draw near to us this day in thine undeserved kindness,—visit us with that love which thou bearest unto thine own.

We are receiving, morning after morning, new proofs of thy care—new pledges of thy mercy. Thou art loading us with thy benefits, though we have been ungrateful and unthankful. It is in the name, and trusting in the merits of thy dear Son alone, that we can have any confidence in approaching thee. We rejoice that we have ever a safe shelter at the foot of his cross.

Lord Jesus, stretch forth thy helping hand. Save us, else we perish. There is not a sin but thou canst cancel ;— there is not the unsanctified heart which thy promised spirit is unable to convert into a temple of the living God. Do thou keep us from evil: preserve us from temptation. As good soldiers may we range ourselves under thy banner; animated by holy allegiance to him who is the great captain of our salvation. We would seek to repose on the divine promises. May our weakness drive us to almighty strength. Good Lord, keep us, by thy grace, from an uneven walk, from inconsistency of conduct. May we be gentle, and lowly, meek, and forgiving. May we overcome evil with good.

Do thou bless this family and household. May it be

one of the tabernacles of the righteous, where the voice of joy and melody is often heard.

We pray for all in sorrow; may they look to the hand which was pierced for them, to bind up their bleeding wounds. May he who graciously said of old, "I know their sorrows," be near, with his own exalted sympathy, to minister to their varied experiences of trial.

We pray for thy cause throughout the world. Bless our nation; may it be the honored instrument, among the kingdoms of the earth, in greatly promoting the glory of God. Bless every rank and condition; may thy favor encompass all as with a shield.

May the Lord arise, and have mercy upon Zion. Prince of Peace, take to thyself thy great power and reign! Go forth in thy glorious apparel, travelling in the greatness of thy strength; manifest thyself as "mighty to save." Let thy glorious gospel be everywhere proclaimed, with its sublime messages: May it heal all wounds, and redress all wrongs; may it rescue the tempted, and save the lost!

Be thou with us, blessed Lord, this day. May thine angels encamp round about us and keep us in all our ways; and when we come to die, do thou receive us into everlasting habitations, for the sake of Jesus Christ, our only Savior. Amen.

WEDNESDAY EVENING.

BE ye therefore perfect, even as your Father which is in heaven is perfect.—Matt. v. 48.

Most blessed God, thou giver of all grace, draw thou near to us; enable us to end another day with thee, and to retire to rest, in the conscious possession of thy friendship and love.

What are we, that we should be permitted to approach such a glorious and infinite God! We are dust and ashes, —creatures of a day—who might, long ere now, have been righteously spurned from thy presence. Blessed be thy great and holy name, for all the manifold proofs of thy favor. Thy ways are not as our ways; had they been so, we must all of us have perished without hope. Do thou give to each of us this night, to know the blessedness of being at peace with thee,—of taking hold on that everlasting covenant, which is well-ordered in all things and sure; looking away from our guilty selves and our guilty doings, to him who has done all and suffered all, and procured all for us.

May we feel it to be our joy to serve him, our privilege to follow him, our sorrow to vex and grieve him. Take us and use us for thy glory;—sanctify our affections—elevate our desires. Keep us from being over-careful and over-troubled about earth's many things;—enable us to be more solicitous about the one thing needful; may we be covetous only of the solid and durable riches of eternity.

Bless our beloved relatives; may they all be enabled to claim a common kindred with the one Elder Brother on the throne. Though separated from one another now, may thy blessed angels gather us together, at last, in the same bundle, for the Heavenly Garner.

Let none put off preparation for death till a dying hour:—a present hour is all that we can call our own;—may we be living in that state of holy preparedness, that when the silver cord, by which life is suspended, is broken, we may be ushered into thy presence, and into the enjoyment of glory everlasting.

Look down on thy church everywhere throughout the world;—purify her more and more;—may no weapon formed against her prosper; may her ministers be men of God, and may her saints and people shout aloud for joy. Do thou satisfy Zion's poor with bread. May every afflicted one partake of thine own consolations, and be led meekly to say, "the Lord's will be done."

Graciously take the charge of us during this night. We commend us all to thy fatherly protection and care;—whether we wake or sleep may we live together with thee. And all we ask is for the Lord Jesus Christ's sake. Amen.

THURSDAY MORNING.

PHILIP said unto him, Lord, shew us the Father, and it sufficeth us. Jesus said unto him, He that hath seen me hath seen the Father.—John xiv. 8, 9.

O Lord, we desire to approach the footstool of thy throne, adoring thee as the everlasting God, the Lord, the Creator of the ends of the earth, who faintest not, neither art weary. Thy wisdom never fails—thy resources never exhaust. The kindness of the kindest knows a limit, but thy kindness knows no limit. With thy friendship, and favor, and blessing we are rich, whatever else thou mayest take away. Change is written on all around us—time may estrange the nearest and dearest on earth, but "thou art the same;"—loving us at the beginning, thou wilt love us unto the end.

We come unto thee this morning in the name of thy dear Son. Our sins reach unto the clouds—we cannot answer for one of a thousand; but we rejoice that we can look up to him who *has* answered for us. Blessed Savior, we would bury all our transgressions in the depths of thy forgiving mercy. We *seek* no other refuge, and *need* no other refuge, but thee. Relying on thy finished work, we can look calm and undismayed on the unknown future. We can cast all our cares, as they arise, upon thee, feeling not only that thou carest for us, but that thou makest these cares thine own. We can look forward to the last enemy —to death inself, without alarm; the rays of thy love will disperse the gloom of the dark valley, and cause us to rejoice in hopes full of immortality.

Sanctify thy providential dealings to the sons and daughters of affliction. May they come forth from the furnace. purified as gold. Spare useful and valued lives; and may those appointed to death fall sweetly asleep in Jesus, in the sure and certain hope of a resurrection to eternal life.

Bless thy church everywhere; may all its ministers be men of God, valiant for the truth; warning every man, and teaching every man in all wisdom. Sustain the faith of those, who, amid manifold discouragements, are laboring in heathen lands: may the Lord send his angel to stand by them, and to shut the mouth of every gainsayer. Hasten that glorious time, when the year of thy redeemed shall come, and the whole earth shall be filled with thy glory.

Bless all of us who are here assembled. Known unto thee are our several wants, and temptations, and perplexities. Make thy grace sufficient for us. May a sense of thy presence hallow all the day's duties, and lighten all its trials. Go with us where we go: dwell with us where we dwell. May the peace of God, which passeth all understanding, keep our hearts. And all we ask is for the sake of him whom thou hearest always—Jesus Christ, our only Lord and Savior. Amen.

THURSDAY EVENING.

A S the Father hath loved me, so have I loved you: continue ye in my love.—John xv. 9.

Most blessed Lord, Father of all mercies, thou art from everlasting to everlasting God; the same yesterday, and to-day, and forever. During the past day, many of our fellow-beings have gone into eternity;—we are spared. Thou hast been compassing our path—shielding us from danger, and guarding us from temptation. None is so able, none is so willing, as thou art, to befriend and guide us in every perplexity.

We desire this night to retire to rest, in the assured confidence of thy favor. Forgive all the sins of the past day—its sins of omission and commission,—of thought, and word, and deed;—whatever has been inconsistent with thy pure and holy will. Make us more zealous for thy honor and glory;—may we maintain a constant and habitual hatred of those sins which have so long severed us from thee.

Bless all who are in affliction. May they be led to lean confidingly on the arm of Jesus, and they shall be more than conquerors.

We pray for the whole world. Pity the nations that are sunk in heathen darkness. May they know thee, as a prayer-hearing, a prayer-answering, a covenant-keeping God. Direct their hearts into thy love, and into the patient waiting for Christ.

Own every means for the promotion of thy cause. May the divine Dove of Peace brood, as he did over chaos of old, bringing light out of darkness, and order out of confusion. May we all feel, in our varied spheres of influence, that we have some mission, however lowly, to perform for thee, and for the good of others. Give the single eye, and the single aim, and the lofty unalloyed motive.

Bless our household. May the joy of the Lord be our strength. May we feel that in keeping thy commandments there is a great reward. As the pillar of cloud goes before us by day, may the pillar of fire be with us by night. May angels gather around us during the unconscious hours of sleep;—may no danger befall us, and no plague come nigh our dwelling. If pleased to spare us till to-morrow, may we rise fitted and prepared for all the duties to which we may be called.

And now unto him who alone is able to keep us from falling, and to present us faultless before the presence of his glory with exceeding joy, to the only wise God and our Savior, be ascribed all blessing and honor, dominion and praise, world without end. Amen.

FRIDAY MORNING.

I N my Father's house are many mansions . . I go to prepare a place
for you.—John xiv. 2.

Almighty and most merciful Father, thou art great and
greatly to be feared; thy greatness is unsearchable. Thou
art infinite in wisdom, and power, and love; thy justice is
as the great mountains, thy judgments are a great deep.

Lord, our hearts are by nature deceitful above all
things and desperately wicked. We have done those things
we ought not to have done, and we have left undone those
things which we ought to have done, and there is no health
in us. Have mercy upon us, for his sake, in whom thou
seest no iniquity. We have nothing of our own but our
sins; all that is good in us comes from him; we would confidently repose cur everlasting interests on his finished
work.

May it be our lofty aim to be the servants of righteousness: may we show that the influence of thy goodness and
loving-kindness is to lead us to repentance,—to reclaim
our hearts from their wanderings, and bring them into captivity to the obedience of Jesus. We desire to take him in
all things as our pattern. When in want of direction or
guidance in any duty, or under any perplexity, may this be
ever our inquiry—how would the Savior have acted here?
May life be a more constant effort than it has been, to cru-
cify self and to please God. Let us be willing to accept of
anything with thy approval, and to dread nothing but what

incurs thy wrath and displeasure. In our varied spheres may we seek to feel that we have *some* work to perform—*some* talent to trade on. Let us cast by faith our mites into thy treasury, that we may earn at last this thine own meed of approbation,—" They have done what they could."

Let thy hand be around all our beloved friends, present or absent. Inscribe their names in the Lamb's Book of Life; may they be thine on that day when thou makest up thy jewels. Sanctify sorrow to the sons and daughters of affliction; let them not murmur under thy Fatherly chastisements; let them own thy Sovereignty, and take comfort in the thought that thou doest all thing well.

We commend us, blessed Lord, to thee, and to the word of thy grace. Do thou hear, answer, and accept of us, for the sake of him who thou hearest always, and to whom, with thee, the Father, and thee ever blessed Spirit, —Three in One, in covenant for our redemption,—be ascribed all blessing, and honor, and glory, and praise, world without end. Amen.

FRIDAY EVENING.

IS Ephraim my dear son? is he a pleasant child? for since I spake
against him, I do earnestly remember him still . . I will surely
have mercy upon him, saith the Lord.—Jer. xxxi. 20.

O Lord, we desire to approach thy throne of grace,
thanking thee for the liberty of access we at all times enjoy
into thy presence.   We bless thee that the gates of prayer
are ever open ;—that thou regardest the cry of the needy,
and never sayest unto any of the seed of Jacob, " Seek ye
my face in vain."

Blessed Jesus, thou great covenant angel, let down thy
golden censer into the midst of us this night, that we may
have these our petitions perfumed with the incense of thine
adorable merits.   In thee alone are our persons and our
services rendered acceptable.   We flee to the foot of thy
cross.   Here we are safe, though everywhere else we be in
danger.   Let us exercise a simple confidence and trust in
thy completed work.   We bring every sin to thy atoning
blood—every wound to thy healing.   May we have thee
in all, and *for* all the duties and difficulties and trials of
life.   Do thou disarm all its crosses—sanctify its losses :—
may prosperity and adversity be alike used for thy glory.

Let us hate evil;—keep us especially from presumptuous sins, let them not have dominion over us.   Loving
thee our God, may we love our fellow-men ; may we be
patient and unselfish, forbearing and forgiving, lowly and
meek, pitiful and courteous.   Let us overcome evil with
good.   May all our things be done with charity.   May we

show, by our Christ-like walk and conversation, what spirit we are of; not conformed to the sinful practices and base compliances of a world lying in wickedness,—but seeking to have our conduct moulded in conformity with thy holy will.

Thou sympathising Savior, be the friend of the friendless; the support and solace of the bereaved. There are nameless sorrows on earth which are beyond the reach of the tenderest human sympathy—blessed Jesus, thou knowest their sorrows. Let all thy tried people with joy anticipate that gladsome morning, when the shadow of death shall be merged in eternal glory.

Bless our beloved friends;—may thy loving eye rest upon them; may a sense of thy favor pervade all their doings. May none be found wanting at thy right hand, on the great day.

Let us seek to order our plans as dying creatures. Night after night, as we retire to rest, may we think of that deeper darkness, which must, sooner or later, gather around us. Shepherd of Israel, who never slumbers and never sleeps, be thou very near us. As we now retire to rest, may we repose in thy keeping; and in the morning, when we rise, may we rise refreshed for duty,—fitted for whatsoever may be in store for us.

Hear us, blessed God, and grant us an abundant answer, for the sake of him whom thou hearest always. Amen.

SATURDAY MORNING.

L ET your light so shine before men, that they may see your good works, and glorify your Father which is in heaven.—Matt. v. 16.

O Lord, we desire to come into thy blessed presence on this the morning of a new day, adoring thee for all thy mercies. Last night we might have slept the sleep of death; we might have been startled by the midnight cry, "Prepare to meet thy God!" But thy love and forbearance again permit us to meet on praying ground; the day of grace is lengthened, and the God of grace waits to be gracious.

Lord, we look back with amazement at thy patience. Mercies have been abused —providences slighted—warning neglected. Our lives contain a long retrospect of ingratitude and guilt.

But thou art not willing to leave us in our state of estrangement and sin. Thou art ever opening up a way for the return of thy prodigal wayward children. In wrath thou art remembering mercy. We have still the richest encouragement to repair to the opened fountain; Jesus still waits—his blood still cleanses—his spirit still pleads. The faithful saying is as faithful as ever—" Him that cometh unto me I will in no wise cast out."

We desire to receive this new day as a fresh gift from thee. Let thine approval form, throughout it, a holy incentive to every duty. Let us feel that we never can be happy but when pleasing thee. Let us be aiming at a conquest of self; subordinating all we do to thy will and service. We look to thy grace to enable us thus to will and to do. Thou hast wrought all *for* us, and thou alone canst work all *in* us. Strengthen us with might by thy Spirit in the inner man. How slow we are to believe that our truest security is leaning confidingly on thine arm. Thou art faithful that promised. Thy name is the God of *all* grace: thou givest all sufficiency in *all* things. The cup runneth over that is filled by thee—and nothing can come wrong to us that comes from thy hand.

Bless all near and dear to us: all that is truly good for them, in this life, do thou bestow; and, what is better, do thou give them the heritage of glory.

· Take us all, young and old, this day under thy protection. God of all mercy, spread thy covering wings around us. Be our God and guide even unto death, and finally bring us to thine everlasting kingdom through the merits of thy dear Son, our only Lord and Savior, to whom be dominion, power and glory, now and evermore. Amen.

SATURDAY EVENING.

THE father said to one of his servants, Bring forth the best robe, and put it on him; and put a ring on his hand, and shoes on his feet.—Luke xv. 22.

O Lord, thou art the King eternal, immortal, and invisible. The heaven of heavens cannot contain thee. Myriads of pure and holy spirits cease not day nor night to celebrate thy praises.

What are we, that we should be permitted to approach the presence of a God so great and so glorious, and who is of purer eyes than to behold iniquity? We are apt to forget sin, we are too willing to hide it from thee, and to hide it from ourselves; but we cannot evade thy righteous scrutiny. We cannot screen our guilt from the Great Heart-searcher: —all things are naked and open unto the eyes of him with whom we have to do.

But blessed be thy name, though thou art the greatest and the holiest of all beings, thou art also the kindest and most forgiving. Who is a God like unto our God, that pardoneth iniquity! Confiding our eternal all to him, we can rejoicingly say—return unto thy rest, O our souls, for the Lord hath dealt bountifully with us.

Bring us to live more constantly and habitually under the constraining influence of redeeming love. May these souls of ours, ransomed at such a price, be dedicated to thy service. Forbid that any of us should be content with a mere name to live, if we are dead, and deceive ourselves with the form of godliness. Let us know, more and more, that this is thy will concerning us, even our sanctification. May we grow in grace.

Have mercy on all who are in affliction. O thou healer of the broken-hearted, thou helper of the helpless, may every wounded spirit be bound up by thee. May the lonely and unbefriended feel, that in the loneliest solitude, they are not alone, if thou, their God and Father, art with them. Spare valued and valuable lives; and may those who are appointed to death, have the valley-gloom lighted with Immanuel's love.

And now, Lord, what wait we for? Our hope is in thy mercy. Be thou with us this night. Be the guardian of our unconscious hours. Whether we wake or sleep, may we live together with thee. Our wishes, our desires, our interests, our joys, our sorrows, our friends, we leave entirely to thy care and disposal. Prepare us for the solemn duties and services of another day of the Son of man. Give to all of us a double portion of thy Holy Spirit, that our souls may be fitted for holding nearer and more intimate fellowship with thee. And all that we ask is for the sake of him who is the resurrection and the life, and who with the Father and the Holy Spirit, ever liveth and reigneth, world without end. Amen.

SUNDAY MORNING.

A ND it shall come to pass, that in the place where it was said unto
them, Ye are not my people ; there shall they be called the
children of the living God."—Romans ix. 26.

This is the day which the Lord hath made; we will
rejoice and be glad in it. Save now, we beseech thee, O
Lord; O Lord, we beseech thee, send us now prosperity.

This day of holy rest is thy gift to us; thou hast ordained it for us, for special good to our souls. Bless to us
thy gift. As thou dost call us to day from work and from
worldly pleasures, incline us gladly to obey thy call, and to
give this day to thee and to spiritual things, and to seek
thee with all our hearts. All through the day we are now
beginning may we remember thee, and find thee near to us.

Be with us in our private moments, and grant us to
hold communion with thee by the Spirit. Be with us when
we meet in thy house. Bless us, and all the congregation.
Pour out thy Spirit upon us there. Draw our hearts up to
thee in prayer and praise. Speak to us by thy holy Word.
Give us teachable hearts, and make us to feel the power of
thy Word. May we, and all our fellow-worshippers, worship thee in truth, and hear thy Word with profit and comfort.

Give thy presence and blessing to all who may be kept
to-day from thy house; visit them with thy saving grace.
Have compassion on those who wilfully neglect thee and
thy day, and turn away from the house of prayer. O thou,
who didst come to seek and to save that which was lost,

still continue thy gracious work, and in thy mercy seek out this day some who are out of the way.

Look in mercy upon the world at large—upon the Jews, and upon the millions of the heathen. This day bless the work of missions. Be with thy servants abroad, as with us at home. Cheer their hearts, keep them steadfast in the faith, and strong in hope and trust; and bless their work to the gathering in of many souls, and to the futherance of thy glory.

All through this day may we have a sweet savor of thy presence. Be with us in private as well as in public; help us to guard our words and our thoughts, and to keep near to thee in heart.

Visit with thy special grace and blessing all whom we love, those near and those far away. Make this day to them, as well as to us, a day of peace and profit; and may we and they meet in spirit before thee.

Lord, let thy kingdom come! May each one of us be so living as to advance thy kingdom in the world. This day help us to adorn the doctrine of God our Savior in all things. Shed over us a holy calm. Make us to be glad in thee. And whatever we have to do this day in thy service, may we do it with a willing heart, in faith and love, looking to thee for grace and blessing. We ask all for our Savior's sake. Amen.

SUNDAY EVENING.

WHATSOEVER ye shall ask of the Father in my name, He will give it you."—John xv. 16.

O gracious and loving God and Father, we come together now, to thank thee for the mercies of this day. We called upon thee, and thou didst hear us; we sought thee and thou didst not withhold thy blessing from us.

Yet how full of infirmity has our worship been! How poor have been our thoughts, how cold our hearts, how feeble our prayers and praises; and, while we heard thy Word, how far short did we come of what the hearers of the Word should be! If thou shouldest bless us only as we pray, if thou shouldest teach us only according to our hearing, how poor would our blessing be, and how little should we learn! But we pray thee to bless and teach us, not according to our prayers and hearing only, but according to the riches of thy grace in Jesus Christ our Savior. Look upon us in him, and for his sake grant us the fulness of thy saving grace.

Lord, we pray thee to cause thy word to abide within us. Soon we shall have to mingle again with the world, and much there will be to draw away our minds, and make us forget; do thou help us to remember thy Word, and cause it to be a living Word within us.

Forgive every fault thou hast seen in us. At the close of this holy day, as well as on every common day, we need the blood of sprinkling. Lord, take away from us every stain, and grant us now acceptance and peace in Christ our Savior.

Forgive every fault and shortcoming. If our minds have wandered in worship, if we have forgotten thy presence, if light and vain thoughts have crept in, if there has been any lack of serious and earnest attention to thy Word, pardon us for our Redeemer's sake. May his precious blood cleanse us from every stain, and may we lie down to rest accepted in him.

If any here or elsewhere have this day been struck anew by thy Word, or have for the first time felt its power, graciously send down thy Holy Spirit, and confirm the work. Let not the seed be plucked away; let not the heart grow cold and careless again; let not those thoughts pass away.

We now commend ourselves to thee for the night. Take care of us, and of all whom we love. Watch by the bed of the sick, be near to the lonely and sorrowful; keep us and them under the shadow of thy wing. Hear us for our Redeemer's sake. Amen.

MONDAY MORNING.

BUT thou, when thou prayest, enter into thy closet, and when thou hast shut thy door, pray to thy Father which is in secret; and thy Father which seeth in secret shall recompense thee.—Matt. vi. 6.

O Lord our God, we come to thee to thank thee for thy preserving care, and to seek thy blessing for another day. Our help cometh from thee alone: keep us by day as well as by night; this day preserve us in our going out and coming in.

We are now entering on another day: we depend upon thee for all things, by day as well as by night; for we are the creatures of thy hand. This day bless us; guide, uphold, and defend us; of thy bounty supply our various wants; give us thy Holy Spirit; keep us under the shadow of thy wing; and help us in all that we have to do.

Save us from pride and self-confidence; teach us to feel our dependence on thee; make us always humble and trustful. Help us to realize things unseen, and to walk by faith. May we know thy voice, and follow thee.

Give us grace to begin the day, earnestly desiring to do thy will. Put right thoughts and purposes into our hearts. Make it our chief desire and aim, not to please ourselves, but to please thee. May thy Holy Spirit this day dwell within us, and turn our hearts from evil, and incline us to that which is holy and right.

Lord, let not this day be to any of us a wasted day. Give us grace to use it well. Be pleased to employ us in thy service. May thy service be delightful to us, never let us find thy commandments grievous, make us to love thy will and thy work.

Bless our dear relations and friends, bless all who have ever shown us kindness, forgive and bless any who have done us harm in word or deed; bless this place in which we live; bless our country. Guide all who rule in the land: may they rule in thy faith and fear. Put forth thy mighty power against all that is evil; against drunkenness, and Sabbath-breaking, and unbelief, and vice, and crime. Give great success to the Gospel; bless all who minister in it; may sinners be converted unto thee.

Graciously look upon the poor. In thy mercy and loving-kindness provide for their wants, and incline the hearts of others to care for them. May the earth bring forth food for man; may want and distress be kept from us and all; of thy goodness send us such things as we need.

These our prayers and praises we humbly offer in the name of Jesus Christ, our Mediator and Advocate. Amen.

MONDAY EVENING.

HAVING predestinated us unto the adoption of children by Jesus Christ to himself, according to the good pleasure of his will. —Ephesians i. 5.

Lord, we beseech thee now to solemnize our minds. Help us by thy Holy Spirit to draw near to thee truly by Jesus Christ.

We have been brought to the end of another day— another day of mercy and blessing. We thank thee for all thou hast given to us and done for us to-day. We thank thee for thy constant care for our wants.

And we give thee thanks for still continuing to us thy holy Word, and still letting us pray to thee; we praise thee for the open way we enjoy to thy throne of grace, and for an all-prevailing Intercessor. Our sins and shortcomings are many, yet thou dost bless us still; many are the evils thou dost behold in our land, yet thou dost not withdraw thy loving-kindness from us.

We come to seek thy forgiveness. Let not one unpardoned sin remain upon us this night. Pardon us for all that conscience tells us has been wrong, and for all the sins and shortcomings that we ourselves have scarcely noticed, but which have all been seen and known by thee.

Pour out upon us, O Lord, we beseech thee, a spirit of repentance; humble us before thee, as a people. Preserve to us still the light of thy Word, and purity of doctrine, and a faithful ministry. Grant to all thy servants grace to adorn their profession, and to shine as lights in the world. Turn many to righteousness.

Forgive every fault or sin thou hast seen in us to-day, —all sins against thee, and all offences against each other. Cleanse our conscience from guilt by our Savior's precious blood. Teach us even by means of our own transgressions. Make us more humble and watchful.

O thou who neither slumberest nor sleepest, preserve us this night from all evil. Keep us from outward harm, and keep us from all vexing thoughts and recollections, from wrong imaginations, from unholy dreams. Make us to sleep in peace.

To thy gracious protection we commend ourselves and all whom we love, far and near, through Christ our Lord.

The peace of God, which passeth all understanding, keep our hearts and minds in the knowledge and love of God, and of his Son Jesus Christ our Lord: and the blessing of God Almighty, the Father, the Son, and the Holy Ghost, be amongst us, and remain with us always. Amen.

TUESDAY MORNING.

T HEN shall the righteous shine forth as the sun in the kingdom of their Father.''—Matt. xiii. 43.

O Lord our God, again we seek thy face, again we call upon thee in our Savior's name. Hear us now, and for his sake come and be in the midst of us.

We praise thee for thy condescending goodness. What are we, that thou shouldest be mindful of us? Yet thou dost invite us to seek thee, and dost assure us of thy readiness to hear and bless us. We humbly believe thy Word; and now we come before thee and plead thy promises.

We gratefully own thy fatherly care. We thank thee for the sleep thou hast given us. We thank thee for the morning light. Shine into our hearts by thy Spirit. May the Son of Righteousness arise upon us with healing in his beams. Give us spiritual light.

Bless us this day as a household. May we walk together in love. May no provoking words be spoken among us, no harsh or angry spirit be shown, no sullen temper be indulged. Keep us from envy and jealousy, from unkindness and selfishness. Heavenly Father, do thou dwell among us this day, and may thy presence bring us peace.

Bless those we love, who are absent from us. May we and they meet to-day before thy throne. Make us all one in Christ our Lord; and, though absent in the body, may we and they be present with each other in spirit. Help us to remember one another before thee.

Teach our hearts by the reading and hearing of thy Word. Bless to us the daily reading of it in the family. May thy Holy Spirit be with us in our family worship, and make it to be a spiritual service.

This day enable us to walk by faith. We gratefully own thy care of us through the night; we commit ourselves to the same loving care for the day we are now beginning. Prepare us to meet whatever may come to us, Let us not be surprised into sin. Make us watchful and prayerful, may we be found clad in the whole armor of God, and thus may we be enabled to stand.

Whatever our hands find to do this day, may we do it with our might. May our hearts be set to do thy holy will. Make us to love thy will and thy service; and all that we do, may we do unto thee.

We commend ourselves and all dear to us to thy guidance and protection for the day. Go before us by thy grace, and prepare the way for us to walk in; keep us from falling, and from going astray; order all things for us; leave us not, neither forsake us, O God of our salvation.

Peace be to the brethren, and love, with faith, from God the Father and the Lord Jesus Christ. Grace be with all them that love our Lord Jesus Christ in sincerity. Amen.

TUESDAY EVENING.

THAT ye may be the children of your Father which is in heaven."
Matt. v. 45.

Now therefore ye are no more strangers and foreigners, but fellow-citizens with the saints, and of the household of God."—Eph.ii.19.

Lord, be present with us in our evening prayer; help us now to believe that thou art near.

We bow before thee in reverence. We adore thee for thine infinite greatness and majesty. We praise thee for thine unspeakable goodness. We see thee not, yet all around us speaks of thee, and all thy works praise thee, and thy Word declares thee, and thy Holy Spirit testifies of thee in our hearts.

Every day thou dost bless us anew; this day we have received fresh gifts from thy hand: our wants have been supplied, no evil has befallen us, we are still preserved in health and safety. Thine eye has been over us for good; thou hast been with us.

We thank thee for the manifold blessings of our lot; for this peaceful home, for food and raiment, for such a measure of health as thou hast been pleased to give us, for our many personal and family comforts. We thank thee that our lot is cast in a Christian land, that we were not born heathen people, and that even now we are worshipping thee as our God and Father, while so many still know thee not.

Lord, make us to care for others; give us love to all for thy sake; especially give us a deep pity for the heathen. Thou hast taught us to pray that laborers may be sent into

thy harvest; O Lord of the harvest, look in mercy upon
the millions who know thee not, and send forth more laborers into thy harvest. Raise up fit men to go, prepare them
for the work, provide the means, remove difficulties, and
shed abroad a missionary spirit in us all.

Graciously take away the reproach, that many who go
from this country to heathen lands to hinder the Gospel by
their evil lives. Lord, suffer not this shame to remain.
Put forth the power of thy grace on those who leave our
shores, as well as on the heathen. Let not Satan prevail to
hinder thy great work.

Forgive us, if we have ever hindered thy cause by
inconsistency of conduct; forgive us for anything that has
been wrong in us this day—any wrong thought, or word,
or action,—any neglected duty, any opportunity missed.
We cast ourselves, all unworthy as we are, upon thy mercy
in Christ Jesus. Hear us, forgive us, bless and keep us,
for his sake.

Now unto him who is the blessed and only Potentate,
the King of kings and Lord of lords, who only hath immortality, dwelling in the light which no man can approach
unto, whom no man hath seen nor can see, be honor and
power everlasting. Amen.

WEDNESDAY MORNING.

SO Christ was once offered to bear the sins of many ; and unto them that look for him shall he appear the second time without sin unto salvation.—Heb. ix. 28.

O Lord, thou hast been mindful of us, thou hast blest us. We give thee thanks that thou hast kept us from harm through the night, and given us rest.

Heavenly Father, we come to thee now as thy children, seeking thy help and blessing for another day. Every opening day is an unknown day to us, but thou knowest and orderest all. Order all things for us this day, overrule everything for our good, prepare us for whatever may come, guide and strengthen us to pass this day according to thy will.

Prepare us for all that this day may bring—for any news that may reach us ; for any duty thou mayest appoint for us ; for any difficulty, perplexity, or temptation that may arise. Make thy way plain before us, and give us grace to walk therein, and to show a Christian spirit in everything.

It is our happiness to know that we are in thy hand. Thou, Lord, hast never failed them that seek thee. If not a sparrow falleth to the ground without thee, thou wilt never overlook us or our wants. Thou wilt feed us with food convenient for us ; thou wilt watch over us for good ; thou wilt compass us about with thy favor as with a shield. Unworthy as we are, thou wilt bless us for our Savior's sake, because we trust in thee.

We thank thee that thou hast given us thy Word, to teach us of thee. We thank thee for the full liberty we enjoy, to read thy Word, and to worship thee, none making us afraid. If any, in any part of the world, are now suffering persecution for the truth's sake, be thou, O Lord, their helper and comforter. Keep them faithful; help them to glorify thee.

We pray for the spread of the Bible everywhere. Give thy blessing to this great work. May thy Holy Book be in every house in our land, and may every distant people and race have it in their own tongue. May its influence be felt more and more; open the hearts of men to receive it; may it be more read, and loved, and followed.

This day may thy blessing rest upon this house; and not upon us at home only, but also upon all who have gone away from us, and all who are dear to us everywhere. To thy fatherly care and guidance we commend ourselves and them. Keep us all from evil; preserve us from the enemy of our souls. Give to us all thy sanctifying spirit.

Hear us in these our prayers, and send us all else that thou seest we need, for Jesus Christ's sake. Amen.

WEDNESDAY EVENING.

THE Spirit itself beareth witness with our spirit, that we are the children of God : And if children, then heirs ; heirs of God, and joint-heirs with Christ ; if so be that we suffer with *him*, that we may be also glorified together.—Romans viii. 16, 17.

O God, the day has come to a close, and we thy servants once more keeel down together before thee. Let thy loving favor rest upon us, for our Redeemer's sake. Draw us near to thee ; make us all of one mind in seeking thee. May every heart be now truly lifted up to thee.

Thanks be to thee for the mercies of the day. Keep us always mindful of thy goodness. Whether we eat or drink, or whatsoever we do, may we do all in the name of the Lord Jesus, giving thanks unto thee, our God and Father, by him. May all that we enjoy be sweetened to us, as coming from our Father's hand.

Give us serious minds ; help us to live thoughtfully. So teach us to number our days, that we may apply our hearts unto wisdom. May old and young be seeking the one thing needful, and pressing toward the mark.

Lord, teach us to love thee more. We are apt to grow cold and careless : deliver us from hardness of heart, quicken us by thy Spirit, cause us to grow in grace. Enter not into judgment with us on account of our sins, for we cannot answer for one in a thousand. Though thou mightest justly be displeased with us, yet for our Savior's sake look upon us in thy pardoning mercy, and blot out all our transgressions.

Give us more of the mind of thy children. When we call upon thee as our Father, help us to feel the words we say, and really to approach thee as our reconciled and loving Father in Christ Jesus. Let not our prayers now or at any time, be an empty form, let us not render to thee a cold and heartless service ; incline our hearts to pray, give us earnest desires, pour out upon us the Spirit of grace and of supplication, and draw us to thee in faith and love.

The darkness is closing around us ; but the darkness is no darkness with thee. All through the night be thou near us. Give thine angels charge over us, to keep us. May we lie down and sleep, and awake, because thou, O Lord, sustainest us.

Be near this night to all whom we love. Be with the sick and sorrowful everywhere ; comfort all who pass the night in pain ; give peaceful thoughts to those who cannot sleep.

Hear us, O Lord our God, for Christ our Savior's sake.

Now the God of peace, that brought again from the dead our Lord Jesus, that great Shepherd of the sheep, through the blood of the everlasting covenant, make us perfect in every good work to do his will, working in us that which is well pleasing in his sight, through Jesus Christ: to whom be glory for ever and ever. Amen.

THURSDAY MORNING.

I WILL bless the Lord at all times : his praise shall continually be in
my mouth. My soul shall make her boast in the Lord : the humble shall hear thereof, and be glad. O magnify the Lord with me, and
let us exalt his name together.—Psalms xxxiv. 1-3.

O Lord our God, who dwellest on high, and yet hum-
blest thyself to behold the things that are in heaven and in
the earth, we beseech thee now to look down upon us with
favor and acceptance in Jesus Christ our Savior.

May thy name be praised, from the rising of the sun
unto the going down of the same. May the light of the
Gospel shine upon the nations that sit in darkness. Millions, alas, are now beginning the day without thee: O send
out thy light and thy truth, and visit all the heathen with
thy salvation.

Lord, what are we, that thou shouldest have blest us
above so many? Yet bless us now still further; bless us
with a spirit of gratitude and love; teach us to feel how
much we owe; give us a sense of our responsibility; grant
us grace to adorn the doctrine of Christ our Savior; and
make us zealous to make known his saving name.

We thank thee for thy protecting care. O be thou
with us still; by day, as well as by night, guard us from
harm and evil. Especially keep us this day from all sin.
Give us thy Holy Spirit to teach and sanctify us.

May we all be rooted and built up in Christ. Confirm us
in the faith; may nothing draw us away from the simplicity
that is in Christ, from guileless simplicity of heart towards

him. Keep us from being shaken or disturbed by false doctrines, or by any evil example or influence.

Teach us to know ourselves. Let us never be vain or proud. Make us truly humble before thee and towards all. Preserve us from hastiness of temper and from gloom and sullenness. Give us a spirit of cheerful kindness. Keep us from sins of the tongue; set a watch, O Lord, before our mouth; keep the door of our lips.

Help us to live thoughtfully. Let none of us be unprepared to meet thee. That which our Lord said to all, may we have grace to hear and obey; help us to *watch*, that when he comes we may be ready to receive him with joy. This day may we be as servants who wait for their Lord.

Incline our hearts to love thee. May we know and believe the love that thou hast to us; and may we all love thee, because thou didst first love us.

Heavenly Father, look with favor upon this house to-day; and upon all whom we love, wherever they may be. May we and they be safe in thy keeping, and walk by thy guidance, and serve thee truly, and do thy holy will.

Peace be to the brethren, and love, with faith, from God the Father and the Lord Jesus Christ. Grace be with all them that love our Lord Jesus Christ in sincerity.

Hear us and bless us, for our Redeemer's sake. Amen.

THURSDAY EVENING.

I WILL sing of the mercies of the Lord forever: with my mouth will I make known thy faithfulness to all generations.—Psalms lxxxix. 1.

Lord, what shall we render to thee for all thy grace and goodness? O fill our hearts with gratitude and love. Thou dost need nothing at our hands, yet thou dost condescend to receive honor from our thanks and praises. Give us a heart to praise thee.

Again thou hast been gracious to us. Another day has brought us new mercies. To thee alone do we owe all that we have had and enjoyed to-day. To thee, O gracious Father, be all the praise.

We can count up many mercies received; but how many have come to us unseen! We thank thee for those we know of, and we thank thee for those we know not of— for any unseen danger this day warded off from us, for any secret guidance, for all hidden blessings.

Let thy pardoning love pass over all the offences of this day. Thou knowest all we have done, and thought, and said. Thine eye has been upon us. Wash us from every stain in our Savior's blood; wash us, and we shall be whiter than snow.

Thou hast graciously taught us to call thee " Father," and bidden us to come to thee as thy children. We gladly come to thee, to put ourselves into thy care for the night. No evil can harm us, if thou be near. Lord, be near us through the dark hours, spread thy wing over us, shelter us from all harm.

We pray for growth in grace. May none of us be loiterers on the way. Quicken us by the power of thy Spirit. May we all, by thy grace, be more deeply serious, more in earnest, more full of love to thee, more spiritual in mind and heart. And may we, as a family, be more and more such as it becomes a Christian household to be. May kindness and love reign here, may a pure and holy tone be the tone prevailing in this house, may the love of the world find no place among us, and may we have grace so to walk that a light may shine from this dwelling to all around.

And what we ask for ourselves, we ask also for all we love. Watch over those who are far away; watch over all who are dear to us. Grant to us and to them that which thou dost give to thy beloved. Grant us sleep. We ask all for our Savior's sake.

The Lord bless us and keep us;

The Lord make his face to shine upon us, and be gracious unto us;

The Lord lift up his countenance upon us, and give us peace.

The grace of our Lord Jesus Christ be with us all.

Peace be to the brethren, and love, with faith, from God the Father and the Lord Jesus Christ. Grace be with all them that love our Lord Jesus Christ in sincerity. Amen.

FRIDAY MORNING.

I SAID, I will take heed to my ways, that I sin not with my tongue: I will keep my mouth with a bridle, while the wicked is before me.—Psalms xxxix. 1.

Help us now, O Lord, to draw near to thee. Incline our hearts to seek thee. And graciously admit us into thy presence, through Jesus Christ.

Give us grace to begin the day with thee. In thy strength may we go forth to do what we have to do. And may we do all, not with eye-service as men-pleasers, but as the servants of Christ, doing the will of God from the heart. We are thy servants: make us faithful and diligent in serving thee.

Give us right views of life and time. The day we are now beginning is a fresh gift from thee. Thou hast preserved us through the night, and caused us to see another day; thou hast kept us still in life and health; and now this day brings us new opportunities of serving thee. May this be now our chief desire—to serve thee and please thee, and do thy will, throughout this day.

Give us right motives. May love to thee be the spring of all we do. Keep us from selfishness, and vanity, and pride, and the love of praise. Make us content to be little thought of, so only we may do that which is pleasing in thy sight.

Keep us from idleness and self-indulgence; let not this day pass without our doing good to some. If nothing else be appointed for us, may we have grace to walk aright, and to show a good example ; and may all our words this day be right words.

Keep us from sin of every kind. Keep us especially from whatever sin we are most prone to. Where we have fallen in time past, there make us doubly watchful ; let no temptation come upon us unawares. Guard our hearts from the evil one. Fill us with the Holy Ghost.

Strengthen us with strength from above. Fill us with the Holy Ghost. Grant us to abide in Christ; and may he dwell in our hearts by faith. In thy strength may we meet all temptation and difficulty that may come to us to-day.

Thou hast set before us a way to walk in, and given us all a place to fill for thee, and talents to use in thy service. Impress upon us our Savior's words, "Occupy till I come." This day may we be found faithful.

Lord, in thy favor is life : let thy loving favor rest upon us to-day as a family, and upon each one of us. Thou knowest our wants, and thou knowest what is best for us. Order all our concerns, guide us in the way, send to us what thou seest to be best. And deal thus, O heavenly Father, not only with us, but with all dear to us, for our blessed Savior's sake. Amen.

FRIDAY EVENING.

REJOICE evermore. Pray without ceasing. In every thing give thanks: for this is the will of God in Christ Jesus concerning you.—1 Thess. v. 16-18.

Again, O heavenly Father, the hours have passed, and the day has come to a close; and again we bend the knee before thee.

Thou hast seen us through the day. Thine eye has marked our steps, thine ear has heard our words, and our most secret thoughts have been open to thee. Gracious Lord, for Jesus Christ's sake, blot out of thy book all that may this day have been written against us. Wash us from every stain in his precious blood, and for his sake cast all our sins behind thee.

What shall we render unto thee for thy goodness? Thou dost preserve us in life day after day, thou dost give us health and safety, thou dost grant to us peace in our dwelling, thou dost bestow upon us food and clothing and all needful things. Above all, thou hast given us the good hope of eternal life in Jesus Christ, and hast provided us with the means of grace, and promised us thy Holy Spirit. Lord, we are in danger of forgetting to thank thee, because thy gifts come to us every day. Keep us from unthankfulness. May daily blessing call forth daily praise. Give us the spirit of praise. Make us thankful.

We would not stand still in the Christian course; we would not be cumberers of the ground: stir up our wills and affections, quicken us by thy Spirit, make us fruitful in heart and life; may each day we live be to us all a day of going forward.

We humbly pray to thee on behalf of others. May all dear to us know thee. May none be wanderers from the fold. If any have gone astray, if any are living without thee, O God of grace, cause thy Word to reach them, fetch them home, draw them to thee in Christ Jesus.

Bless our neighbors and friends. This night may thy protecting care be over them, as well as over us. May the powers of darkness prevail against none of us; may we all be kept safe from outward harm and danger. Gracious Lord, do thou thyself, from heaven thy dwelling-place, watch over us through the night, and grant us a happy waking in the morning.

Lord, as life goes on, make us more thoughtful and diligent, more self-denying, more truly devoted to thee. Help us to give thee the first place in our hearts. And the life which we now live in the flesh, may we live by the faith of the Son of God, who loved us, and gave himself for us.

The Lord bless us and keep us ;

The Lord make his face to shine upon us, and be gracious unto us ;

The Lord lift up his countenance upon us, and give us peace.

The grace of our Lord Jesus Christ be with us all. Amen.

SATURDAY MORNING.

BEHOLD, I stand at the door, and knock: if any man hear my
voice, and open the door, I will come in to him, and will sup
with him, and he with me.—Revelation iii. 20.

O thou, who neither slumberest nor sleepest, our
Keeper by day and by night, we thank thee for having
watched over us, and given us rest. Our help cometh from
thee, who didst make heaven and earth. We now again
lift up our eyes unto thee. Help us, and bless us, this day,
O Lord our God.

Make us to see wisdom and love in all thy dealings
with us. Teach us submission to thy will, and a perfect
contentment with all that thou doest. May prosperity
never make us proud or turn away our hearts from thee;
and in the day of trouble be thou our Refuge. If thou
shouldest chastise us, teach us to feel that thou art dealing
with us as with thy children. Give us continual thankfulness of heart.

Once more our table is spread, and we awake to find
ourselves surrounded with comforts. O thou who art the
giver of all, still be gracious to us in supplying our outward wants; but, above all, visit our souls with thy grace,
and send down upon us the fulness of spiritual blessing.
Increase our desires after thee. May our treasure be above;
and where our treasure is, there may our hearts be also.
We believe that he, who once died for us, now lives for us,
and pleads for us. Heavenly Father, for his sake send to
us thy Holy Ghost to comfort us, draw our hearts up to

thee, even now may we enjoy our Savior's presence by the Spirit and in thine own good time give us a place where he is.

Meanwhile, help us to run with patience the race that is set before us, looking unto Jesus, the author and finisher of our faith. This day help us; for each day is a part of our race, and each day we need to look to him. Prepare us for all that the day may bring. May we be rooted and grounded in Christ. Stablish us in the faith, as we have been taught; and cause us to abound therein with thanksgiving.

We ask for a spirit of kindness and love, among ourselves and towards all. Let none of us this day grieve the Holy Spirit of God. May all bitterness and wrath and anger and clamour and evil speaking be put away from us, with all malice; and make us kind one to another, tenderhearted, forgiving one another, even as thou for Christ's sake hast forgiven us.

Lord, we desire to serve thee; but do thou strengthen the desire. Make us to abhor that which is evil and cleave to that which is good. May our hearts be set upon doing thy holy will in faith and love.

May the dew of thy grace and blessing descend upon us this morning. Before we begin our daily work, send down to us thy Holy Spirit, to guide and comfort and strengthen us.

Lord, hear us, we beseech thee; and send this day to us and to those we love more than we can ask or think, for Christ our Savior's sake. Amen.

SATURDAY EVENING.

THE sea saw it, and fled: Jordan was driven back. The mountains skipped like rams, and the little hills like lambs.—Psalm cxiv. 3, 4.

O Lord God Almighty, our Father in heaven, we sought thee when the day began, and now that thou hast brought us to its close in safety, we kneel down together to give thee thanks, and to commit ourselves to thy care for the night.

Give us now and always seriousness of mind. Teach us to remember that each day that passes brings us so much nearer to our last. May none of us spend our days in idleness or trifling, or put off seeking thee; make us truly wise; incline us all to seek thee while thou mayest be found.

We thankfully acknowledge thy goodness to us—thy bountiful kindness in supplying our wants, thy constant care over us, thy tender dealing with us, thy forbearance and long-suffering. We do not feel thy goodness as we ought: make us to feel it more; teach us to love thee more for all thy grace and loving-kindness towards us.

We acknowledge our manifold transgressions and shortcomings: wash us, O Lord, from our iniquity, and cleanse us from our sin; for our Savior's sake, who paid our debt with his own blood, pardon us for all our offences, and grant us this night acceptance and peace.

Prepare us for the coming Lord's day. Refresh us with sleep, both in mind and in body. Help us now to lay down for awhile the cares and business of life, and to raise

our thoughts to thee. Fix our attention and desires on
spiritual things; and may a sweet foretaste of thy holy day
be given to us now.

We praise thee for our temporal blessings; but lead
us, we beseech thee, to prize yet more highly the spiritual
blessings of thy grace. We thank thee for sending thy Son
to be our Savior, and for teaching us of Him in thy Word,
and for giving us the promise of thy Holy Spirit, and for
granting us the privilege of prayer. Thanks be unto thee,
O God, for thy unspeakable gift!

May that precious blood, of which we have learnt in
thy Word, be now applied to wash away all our sins. For
Jesus Christ's sake, forgive us for every fault of this day.
Blot out, as a thick cloud, our transgressions, and, as a
cloud, our sins; and cause us all now humbly to return
unto thee, because thou hast redeemed us.

And grant the same to all whom we love. Watch
over us and them, and give us all a happy waking on the
day of prayer. We cannot all meet together in the body;
but help us to meet to-morrow in spirit, and, though apart
from one another, yet to worship thee together.

May these our imperfect prayers find acceptance with
thee, O Lord our God, through Jesus Christ, our Mediator
and Advocate.

Now unto him who is able to keep us from falling,
and to present us faultless before the presence of his glory
with exceeding joy; to the only wise God our Savior, be
glory and majesty, dominion and power, both now and
ever. Amen.

SPECIAL OCCASIONS.

CHRISTMAS DAY.

Almighty and everlasting God, the Father of our Lord Jesus Christ, we desire, on this sacred anniversary, to draw near to thee, in his name. Our souls would magnify the Lord—our spirits would rejoice in God our Savior; for he that is mighty hath done great things for us, and holy is his name. Blessed be the Lord God of Israel, for he hath visited and redeemed his people, and hath raised up for us an horn of salvation in the house of his servant David.

We look back with gratitude and joy to that memorable night, when the angels appeared over the Plains of Bethlehem, proclaiming that the promised child was born, the promised Savior was given; that through him, while glory was secured to God in the highest, peace was proclaimed on earth, and good-will to the children of men. We adore thee for that amazing love which brought the Lord of life and of glory from his throne in heaven to that manger of humiliation; " God over all," dwelling in union with an infant of days !

We desire to present ourselves before the Holy Child Jesus, like the wise men of old, with the gold, and frankincense, and myrrh of our best affections and deepest love. Had it not been for this inconceivable stoop from the infinite to the finite, where would we have been this day? Well may we join in the angelic song, and say, " Glory ! eternal glory be to God in the highest, for his best—his unspeakable gift; without which, not one ray of hope or joy could have visited our doomed world." As we gather in thought around his cradle, may our souls rise in lively gratitude to him who spared not his only Son, but freely gave him up unto death for us all. We will sing unto the Lord a new song, for he hath done marvellous things; his right hand and his holy arm have gotten him the victory. Thanks be unto God who giveth us the victory, through the Lord Jesus Christ.

May we seek, by holy, righteous, and consistent lives —to show that we are not insensible of all his unmerited love and kindness. Blessed Jesus, make us thine. Sanctify us wholly :—wean us from earth :—train us for glory. Contemplating thee this day in thy humiliation, when thou wast made in the likeness of man, may it be ours to look forward, with holy joy, to thy second coming in the clouds of Heaven—thy tears, and sorrows, and sufferings all past; —when the Babe of Bethlehem—the sufferer of Gethsemane —the crucified of Calvary—shall be seated on the Throne of universal empire, and crowned "Lord of all."

We pray that thy holy name may be everywhere magnified. Arise, O God, and plead thine own cause. May a dark world be soon cheered by the wondrous proclamation we this day love to recall. May the " Prince of Peace " take to himself his great power and reign ; causing men to beat their swords into plough-shares and their spears into pruning hooks.

Give us all that is really good for us ;—withhold all that is evil. May thy will be our only rule and directory ; may we trust thee in everything ; and look forward with joyful hearts to that better time, when we shall be permitted, with a multitude which no man can number, to take up the song of this day, and ascribe " glory to God in the highest," for that mercy which, through his own dear Son, is to endure for ever. Amen.

THE LAST NIGHT OF THE YEAR.

O Lord, we adore thee as the God of times and seasons, of days, and of years. Thou alone art without any variableness or shadow of turning. Thou didst inhabit the glories of eternity, before the birth of time or of worlds. Thou hadst no beginning of days;—thou canst know no end of years. Amidst fleeting moments and revolving seasons, the past and present and future are, to thee, one ever-persent "Now." A thousand years in thy sight are but as yesterday when it is past, or as a watch in the night. It is our comfort to know, amid so much that is transient in a fleeting world, that thou art the same,—that thy throne has the pillars of immutability to rest upon,—that though all be changing and hastening to decay and dissolution, " *thy* dominion endureth throughout all generations."

We desire, on this the last day of another year, to bow at thy footstool, and to take a solemn retrospect of all the year's mercies. We have indeed good reason this night to set up our Ebenezer, and to say, " The Lord hath helped us." It is a retrospect of love. From how many unseen dangers hast thou delivered us ;—from how many temptations, which we had no strength of our own to resist, hast thou rescued us ! How many during this last year have been wasted with sickness, or racked with pain, or stretched on beds of languishing ; yet thou hast mercifully protected us. How many thousands of our fellow-men, since the year began, have passed into eternity ; but we are preserved another year longer ; night after night we laid ourselves down and slept, because the Lord sustained us, and we are still the objects of thine unceasing watchfulness and tender care.

O God, when we think of thy great mercies, what

shall we say of the retrospect of our past sins? Were we to be judged by the duties and doings, the sins and shortcomings of any one day of the passing year, we would be righteously condemned. Oh, ere the record has passed upwards to thy Great Book, do thou wash out every stain in the blood of Immanuel. We have no hope but in him. We desire this night to hear his own blessed words of consolation and mercy—"Son, daughter, be of good cheer, your sins are all forgiven you." We would mourn the past, and seek for "more grace" for the future. Come, Lord, search us and try us, and see if there be any wicked way in us, and lead us in the way everlasting. May the lives which thou hast, during another year, prolonged and preserved by thy bounty, be willingly consecrated as thank-offerings to thy praise.

We desire, at this time more partieularly, to commend to thy Fatherly care and goodness all in whom we are interested. May our absent friends meet us this night in spirit around the throne of the heavenly grace, severally commending us, as we now desire to commend them, to thy care and love. Make them the objects of thy providential bounty, and the subjects of thy heavenly grace and kingdom.

We desire to retire to rest under the solemnizing impression that we are a year nearer eternity,—that a year more of our probation time is fled,—that a year less of grace and opportunity and privilege belongs to us. Lord, take the charge of us; and if thou art pleased to spare us to see the light of a new day and a new year, may it be to us the emblem of a better morning and a nobler term of being, when earth's shadows and darkness shall have for ever fled, and when we shall be satisfied, awaking in thy likeness. And all we ask is for the Redeemer's sake. Amen.

FIRST MORNING OF A NEW YEAR.

Almighty and everlasting God, thou art the Alpha and the Omega—the first and the last. Amid all the changes of the world, thou changest not. All things below must perish—but thou remainest the same.

Thou hast mercifully preserved us to see the beginning of another year. We desire to begin this new period of our existence by consecrating its hours to thee. We would seek to connect its coming blessings with thee,—to own thy hand and thy wisdom in its coming sorrows; we would seek to feel that it can only be to us a *happy* year by being a *holy* one—spent in thy service and devoted to thy praise.

It is one of the many new years we have seen; we cannot tell how few we may have yet to see. Our prayer is, that we may live this year as if it were to be our last. We desire to take as our motto and superscription throughout its course—"God forbid that we should glory, save in the Cross of the Lord Jesus Christ." Our every temporal comfort, as well as every spiritual blessing, flow to us entirely from Jesus. Oh, do thou enkindle in our hearts a flame of more ardent devotedness to him, whose amazing love it is that crowneth every year with goodness, and makes all its paths to drop fatness. Good Lord, we desire, this morning, to make a fresh consecration of ourselves and our household unto thee. If in past years there has been forgetfulness of thee—if thy kindness has been abused, and thy mercies slighted, and thy name dishonored, enable each and all of us to make this year one of more undivided surrender to thy service. May it be a new year of love, and meekness, and forgiveness, and close walking with God. May sin be more dreaded, and holiness more loved. May the lessons of eternity come more powerfully and impressively home to us. Let us live as immortal beings. Let it not be the impression of a solemn anniversary like the present, but an habitual conviction—"The fashion of this world passeth away."

Good Lord, bless all our dear friends; we would remember them, as we trust they are remembering us, this day, at thy footstool. Hear our mutual prayers: may the cloud of mercy descend on all our heads. Though absent from one another on earth, may faith bring us near, by having our tents pitched by the gate of heaven.

God of all grace, we commend us to thee: undertake thou for us. Let the pillar of thy presence go before us· Do thou direct, control, suggest throughout this year, all that we design or do,—so that every power of our bodies, and every faculty of our souls, may unite for the showing forth of thy praise and glory. And all that we ask is for the sake of Jesus, thine only Son and our Savior. Amen.

GOOD FRIDAY.

O Lord God, our Father, who art in heaven, on this day we look to the cross on Calvary and see what Jesus Christ has suffered to save our souls. He was despised and rejected of men; a man of sorrows, and acquainted with grief. Surely he hath borne our griefs, and carried our sorrows. He was wounded for our transgressions; he was bruised for our iniquities; the chastisement of our peace was upon him; and with his stripes we are healed. He was brought as a lamb to the slaughter; and as a sheep before her shearers, is dumb, so he opened not his mouth.

Help us, O God, to bear in mind, that it was our sins that caused the Savior all that bitter agony, crucifixion and death. Our sins caused him to be rejected and betrayed; our sins caused him the agony in the garden, where his soul was sorrowful, even unto death, and where under the overwhelming burden of the sins of the world, his sweat fell as great drops of blood to the ground; our sins caused him the mockery of his trial, the scourging and the crown of thorns; our sins laid upon him the burden of his cross on the way to Calvary; our sins drove the nails through his hands and his feet, and caused him to exclaim in those awfully mysterious words, My God, my God, why hast thou forsaken me! It was that we might not feel forsaken of God, when we come to die. Help us, O God, to realize the horrible nature of sin, which caused the blessed Savior all that bitter suffering and that cruel death.

God so loved the world that he gave his only begotten Son, that whosoever believeth on him should not perish, but have everlasting life. O God the Father, what shall we render unto thee for thine infinite love to us miserable sinners? O God the Son, how can we ever repay thee for thy dying love. O Lord Jesus, we have nothing that we can truly call our own, but our sins. O take these sins away; wash them away in the fountain of thine atoning blood, the fountain that was opened for sin and uncleanness.

We would make an entire surrender of ourselves to thee. Our bodies and our souls are thine by thy redemption purchase; may they be also thine by the renewing and sanctifying of our hearts by the power of the Holy Ghost.

O thou Lamb of God, that takest away the sins of the world, have mercy on us!

By thy love unto death, even the death of the cross;

By the terrors that encompassed thy soul;

By the sufferings which thou didst endure in thy body;

By the bitter agonies of death, have mercy on us, O Lord Jesus.

And unto him that loved us, and washed us from our sins in his own blood, be glory and dominion for ever and ever. Amen.

EASTER.

THE voice of rejoicing and salvation is in the tabernacles of the righteous; the right hand of the Lord doth valiantly. The right hand of the Lord is exalted, for Christ is risen from the dead. The stone which the builders refused is become the head-stone of the corner—the corner-stone on which God hath erected his everlasting temple. This is the Lord's doing; it is marvellous in our eyes. Enter into his gates with thanksgiving, and into his courts with praise; be thankful unto him, and bless his name. For the Lord is good, his mercy is everlasting, and his truth endureth to all generations. Let us pray:

Glory be to thee, our God, who art, and wast, and shalt be, from everlasting to everlasting. Praise and honour be to thee, the God of our Lord Jesus Christ, the Father of glory; for this is the day which thou hast made for us that we might rejoice and be glad in it. Praise and thanksgiving be to thee, that thy beloved Son appeared among us, not only that he might take away sin by offering himself a willing sacrifice for us, but that he might bring life and immortality to light, and re-open heaven for all who believe in his name. Praise and thanksgiving be to thee for that hidden wisdom, which thou hast ordained so gloriously, beyond all that we could understand or ask. Thou hast not left his soul in the realms of death, nor suffered thy holy one to see corruption. Thou hast fulfilled unto him the promise that thou wouldst show him the path of life, and hast made the captain of our salvation perfect through sufferings. Thanks and praise be to thee, that through the resurrection of Jesus his innocence is established, his dignity made manifest, and his work glorified as thy work; that instead of the crown of thorns, he wears a crown of glory, and that, as the Lord of the living and the dead, he hath received power, as the captain of salvation, to bring many sons unto glory.

Help our infirmities, that with our whole heart we may
rejoice in that glorious gospel which banishes every doubt,
turns our fears into gladness, and ministers unto us abundantly an entrance into the everlasting kingdom of glory·
We praise thee that Jesus was delivered for our offences,
and was raised again for our justification ; and we pray that
we may be made partakers of his resurrection, and thus
walk in newness of life. We rejoice that in thine abundant
mercy, thou hast begotten us again unto a lively hope,
through the resurrection of Jesus Christ from the dead, to
an inheritance incorruptible and undefiled, and that fadeth
not away. Enable us, therefore, to purify ourselves, even
as he is pure, to seek those things that are above, and lay
up treasure in heaven. When temptations assail us, when
our faith would grow weak and our love become cold, do
thou make us steadfast and immovable, always abounding
in the work of the Lord, forasmuch as we know that our
labor is not in vain in the Lord. May all the joys with
which thou crownest our life be increased by the blissful
thought that they are but the foretaste of greater joys to
come. Amidst all the sufferings of our probation, may
we be refreshed by the delightful and consoling conviction
that through them our Father is preparing us for a far more
exceeding and eternal weight of glory. When we mourn
at the graves of those whom we loved, may our hearts
find comfort in the promise that them which sleep in Jesus
will God bring with him. And when we ourselves shall
be called out of this world, may our departing spirit abundantly enjoy that assured hope, by which we are enabled
to say : I know that my Redeemer liveth : O death, where
is thy sting ? O grave, where is thy victory ? Thanks be
to God, who giveth us the victory through our Lord Jesus
Christ. Amen.

ASCENSION DAY.

O Lord Jesus Christ, eternal Son of God, Savior of the world, the King of heaven and of earth, the mighty Conqueror of all our enemies, when thou hadst by thy sufferings and death, accomplished the great work of redemption, thou didst arise from the dead, show thyself alive to thy disciples, give them commandment and bless them, and then ascend up into heaven; thou hast led captivity captive, and given gifts unto men; thou hast spoiled principalities and powers, and made a show of them openly, triumphing over them by thy cross. All power is given unto thee in heaven and in earth. Thou art seated at the right hand of thine everlasting Father, and art exalted above every name that is named, not only in this world, but also in that which is to come. All things are put under thy feet, and thou art the head over all things to the church. The hand-writing of ordinances that was against us has been blotted out, the sentence of condemnation removed, all our guilt cancelled with thy precious blood, and our enemies, death and the devil, have now no more dominion over us. For this thy glorious and mighty victory, we render unto thee most hearty thanks; we praise thee, we worship thee, and humbly beseech thee as our everlasting High Priest, to intercede for us poor sinners with thy heavenly Father, that we, being delivered from all guilt and pain through the merits of thy sufferings and death, may escape the just wrath of God and the punishment of the world to come.

Be gracious unto thy people, and evermore send them thy Holy Spirit. Bless thy church with pious and faithful ministers and officers; preserve us from all errors in doctrine; remove all hinderances to our salvation; protect, establish and extend thy kingdom upon the earth, according to the greatness of thy power, until all thine enemies are laid low at thy feet.

O Thou whose mediation hath brought peace on earth! Give thy peace unto all who obey thy gospel, and according to thy long-suffering have mercy upon unconverted sinners, that they may also renounce the service of folly and sin, and become the children of peace. O thou, who art the author and finisher of the faith of all that believe, and who wast thyself made to enter into thy glory through many sufferings, revive with thine abundant consolation, all who are in affliction or temptation, and arm them with courage and strength from on high, that they may war a good warfare, even unto the end. O thou Prince of life! how many hast thou already cheered and sustained on the bed of death! grant us also thy encouraging and sustaining presence, in the last trying hour of this mortal pilgrimage. When our bodily eyes shall close, grant that with the eye of faith we may behold the gates of heaven open to receive us, and view thee seated at the right hand of God; and graciously hear us, when with our expiring breath, we shall exclaim: Lord Jesus, receive our spirit! O thou Captain of salvation! already hast thou brought many sons to glory; even so lead us also, who still sojourn in this land of mortality and of conflict; enable us, by thy Spirit, to overcome sin, and suffering, and death, and grant us abundantly, through thine atoning merits, an entrance into the kingdom of glory, where thou livest and reignest, in unity of spirit with the Father, in eternal majesty and power. Amen.

WHITSUNDAY OR PENTECOST.

Eternal and exalted God! Thou art the fountain of
life and light and happiness in heaven and on earth! Un-
limited is thy power, unsearchable thy wisdom, inexhausti-
ble thy goodness! With heartfelt emotion we humble ourselves before thy glorious majesty. With thanksgiving
and joy we adore thee as the first and eternal Cause of all
things in heaven and upon earth. On this solemn festival
we bless and praise thee especially for the glorious accomplishment of thy counsel concerning the salvation of mankind. We thank thee with our whole heart, that when
Christ our Saviour had returned to thee, thou didst visit
thy people with new mercies, and establish, by the out-
pouring of thy Holy Spirit, the Church of thy Son upon
earth. Father of our Lord Jesus Christ, be thou exalted in
the congregation of thy people, that thou hast bestowed
this inestimable gift upon sinful men.—With grateful hearts
we cherish the memory of that blessed morn, on which,
through the gifts and powers of thy Spirit, thou didst enlighten and sanctify the first disciples of the Savior, and appoint them to be heralds of peace, and witnesses for the
truth. May all who name the name of Christ, unite in
praising thee; for thy kingdom cannot be moved, and the
Church of thy Son shall endure throughout all generations.
Thou hast given it the seal of thy promise, which is unto
us also, and to our children. Thy Son hath declared, "If
ye, being evil, know how to give good gifts unto your
children, how much more will your heavenly Father give
his Holy Spirit to them that ask him!" Trusting in this
assurance, we beseech thee, in the name of Jesus, to send

him unto us from thy high and holy place, and with him
to grant us all things that pertain to life and godliness.
Grant that we may all be born of the Spirit, that we may
be brought from darkness to light, and translated from the
bondage of corruption into glorious liberty of the children
of God.

Holy Spirit! true and eternal God, with the Father
and the Son, fulfill in us, we beseech thee, this day, thy
mission of love, and abide with us forever. Enlighten and
inspire us with holy zeal and fervency of spirit. Lead us
into all truth.—Enter into us as thy living temples, and
sanctify us wholly in body, soul, and spirit, that we may
not fulfill the lust of the flesh, but walk in all holy obedience and devotion. Deliver us from the law of sin and
death, and anable us to attain unto the liberty and peace of
the saints. Assist us in our prayers, and bear witness with
our spirits that we are the children of God. Seal us according to thy promise, and be thyself the earnest of our inheritance until our redemption be complete.

And now, unto the Father, the Son, and the Holy
Ghost, one God, be all praise, might, worship, and dominion, world without end. Amen.

PRAYER FOR A DAY OF HUMILIATION.

Almighty and most merciful God, thou art glorious in holiness, fearful in praises, continually doing wonders. Thou art of purer eyes than to behold iniquity;—thou canst not look upon sin but with abhorrence. Do thou pour out upon us this day the spirit of grace and of supplication—the spirit of humility and deep abasement. In self-renouncing lowliness we desire to take the publican's place and cry out, " Unclean, unclean!—God be merciful unto us sinners! "

We acknowledge our sins as *individuals*. Our hearts have been estranged from thee;—we have been lovers of pleasure more than lovers of God. Divine things have not been exercising a paramount influence over us. We have been living for earth;—seeking our chief good short of thyself, the only soul-satisfying portion. Our love has been cold—our faith weak—our graces languid;—self and sin have mingled with our best attempts to glorify thee.

We acknowledge our sins as *families*. We have not been exhibiting consistency of walk. Thy Word has not been prized as it ought. The flame of love and devotion has not burned brightly on the domestic altar as it ought. The leaven of vital godliness has not been pervading, with its hallowed influences, our family engagements, and occupations, and duties.

We confess our sins as a *church* and as a *nation*. Lord, thou hast filled our cup with mercies—thou hast dealt with us as thou hast not dealt with any other people. But, alas! have we not abused our privileges? We mourn and blush to think of the vice and profligacy—the intemperance and ungodliness, which is rising up in terrible memorial against our land. We mourn our desecrated Sabbaths, and deserted sanctuaries, and unread Bibles ;—we mourn the eye-service and the lip-homage which, too often among thy professing people, takes the place of heart and soul consecration :—we mourn the little we have done, the much we have left undone, to promote thy cause in the world. Father, forgive us these our many and heinous offences : humble us in the dust because of all our unworthiness. Give us grace this day, while we mourn the past, humbly, but earnestly, to resolve to live more devotedly to thee in the future. Accept of our unworthy confessions, for Jesus' sake. Sprinkle these guilty hearts with his precious blood. Let us seek, in all time to come, to walk before thee in holiness and righteousness of life, to the glory of thy holy name. Amen.

PRAYER FOR A DAY OF THANKSGIVING.

Almighty God! we adore thee as the Father of lights, from whom cometh every good and perfect gift. We come before thee as dependent, frail, and guilty creatures, who cannot exist without thy support, who cannot be happy without thy love. All our powers of mind and body are the work of thy hand. Our outward advantages and enjoyments are the gifts of thy providence, and all our spiritual consolations and improvement flow from thy grace. We bless thee for all those comforts which have sustained and gladdened us in every stage of our pilgrimage. We praise thee, that we are made but a little lower than the angels, and formed with capacities to know, to love, and to rejoice in thee forever. We thank thee, above all for the mission of thy beloved Son, for redemption through his blood, even the forgiveness of sins, for the possession of the precious Gospel, and for the privilege of worshiping thee according to the dictates of our own consciences, none daring to molest us, or make us afraid. What everlasting gratitude is due to thee, that the gospel of thy Son has brought life and immortality to light, that his precepts point out the path of duty, and that his example encourages our works of love! Blessed be thy name, that his death speaks peace and joy to the upright believer, that his resurrection from the grave establishes our confidence in him as our divine Mediator and Redeemer, and that his ascension to glory enlivens our best and earnest hopes!

We entreat thee, for Christ's sake, to be especially mindful of our favoured land; and as thou hast in times past, made thyself known unto us as our God, we pray thee, in times to come, to continue thy favour unto us. Praise be to thee for the liberty that we enjoy ; forbid that it should ever degenerate into licentiousness. Let thine eye be ever open toward this thy people. To this end, inspire the President of the Unted States and all others in authority, with the spirit of wisdom and of thy fear. Grant that through their exertions, peace and unity may be preserved and diffused throughout this Republic, and that they may have the honour of thy name and the extension of the kingdom of thy Son at heart. Grant that the several United States may remain perpetually joined together by the bond of love and peace, that their union may endure to the end of time. We commend· unto thine especial favour the State in which we dwell! May thy Spirit so direct our goverment, that the effect of all its laws shall be the welfare of the citizens. Grant that justice may promptly be administered by our magistrates without respect to persons. Send down upon all ministers and their congregations the needful spirit of thy grace, and give such efficacy to the word of truth and the means of education, that righteousness and peace may be our perpetual inheritance. Grant grace to the people of this land to acknowledge thee as the supreme Governor of the nations, and to dwell together in unity and peace. May those that are young remember their Creator in the days of their youth, and be restrained from the ways of vanity and vice.

And now, what shall we render unto the Lord for all his benefits toward us? How shall we utter the memory of thy great goodness? Open thou our lips, and our mouths shall show forth thy praise ; yea, we will sing unto thee as long as we live.

Glory be to the Father, and to the Son, and to the Holy Ghost, as it was in the beginning, is now, and ever shall be, world without end. Amen.

ANNIVERSARY OF THE REFORMATION.

Adorable and incomprehensible God, thou art the King of kings and Lord of lords, all whose laws are just, and righteous, and good. We thank thee, that when all flesh had corrupted its way, and the earth was filled with violence and sin, thou didst not cast us off from thy presence, but did send thy Son to redeem us from the dominion and the curse of sin. We bless thy name, O God, that thou didst found thy church upon a rock, and promise that the gates of hell shall never prevail against her. We thank thee, for the evidences of thy divine favour, on the labors of thine apostles and ministering servants in the earlier ages. We bless thee, that after the unfaithfulness of men had obscured the light of thy truth, after error, superstition and bigotry had corrupted the heritage of thy Son, thou didst again do good unto Zion in thine own time, and build again the broken walls of Jerusalem. We thank thee, that thou didst, in successive ages, raise up witnesses for the truth. And we bless thee that in due time thou didst send thy servants, the Reformers, and through them didst revive thy church, and restore her primitive purity, and simplicity of doctrine and worship. Thanks be to thee, O God, that we are now permitted to worship thee according to the dictates of our own consciences, none daring to molest us or make us afraid. Lord, it was thy work, and not the work of man. Thou didst raise up those faithful servants, and teach them to see and feel the errors and corruptions of the church. We thank thee, that thou didst enlighten them with the knowledge of thy truth and set them free, that they might bring others to the blessed liberty of Christ Jesus. Thou didst inspire them with courage to stand forth as witnesses to thee, to assail the corruptions which had been brought into thy sanctuary, and not to fear the enmity of the mighty of this world.

Most merciful God, preserve unto us evermore this invaluable blessing, that all generations to come may rejoice in it. Be thou continually the Defender, the Protector, and the Savior of thy church   Enlighten, sanctify and bless her through thy holy word and sacraments. Grant her grace rightly to value the privileges which thou hast bestowed upon her, that she may hold fast what she hath, that no man may take her crown. Purify her from all offences, and graciously defend from all schisms and divisions. We beseech thee, O thou Lord of the harvest, to raise up and qualify, and send forth many more laborers into the field of the world, that they may soon preach the gospel to every creature. Accompany their preaching with the mighty influence of thy Spirit, that sinners may be awakened, that saints may be edified, and thy kingdom be built up in holiness and faith. Help us to stand fast in the liberty wherewith Christ hath made us free, and never suffer us to become the slaves of men or servants of sin. Have mercy, O God, upon all mankind ! Bestow the blessings which we enjoy upon all our brethren, who are destitute of them. Restrain, every where, the kingdom of darkness upon earth, and cause the light of thy truth to shine in all the world. Turn the hearts of those who hate thy word, and pardon their iniquities. Visit with thy saving power all who suffer tribulation, oppression, and persecution, and deliver them by thy mighty arm out of all their troubles. Enlighten and lead back those who have erred and strayed from thee, convince the doubting, strengthen the weak-hearted, and make all thy children meet for their eternal and blissful inheritance, through Jesus Christ our Lord and Savior. Amen.

MORNING OF A COMMUNION SABBATH.

Almighty and everlasting God, we bless thee for the return of another day of the Son of man. May our communion and fellowship this day be with the Father, and with his Son Jesus Christ.

We thank thee for the prospect we have—of surrounding once more the table in the wilderness, and partaking of the bread of everlasting life. Give to each of us the " wedding garment." Let us prepare to meet our God. May we feel that the place whereon we are to stand is holy ground; and rejoice at the renewed opportunity of testifying, in the presence of angels and men, our unaltered and unalterable attachment to our blessed Lord and Master. In a strength greater than our own, may we be enabled to resolve, that he will be henceforth ours, only—ours wholly —ours forever.

Give us this day a lively impression of the great love wherewith he hath loved us. May our faith be strengthened, and our love deepened, and our graces renewed. May this be the grateful aspiration of our hearts—" What shall we render unto the Lord for all his benefits towards us? We will take the cup of salvation, and call upon the name of the Lord; we will pay our vows unto the Lord now in the presence of all his people."

We pray for all who are to commune with us this day at thy table. Give to each of them some special tokens of thy covenant love. May their experience be—" It was good for us to draw near unto God." Keep back all presumptuous and unworthy guests. Encourage all misgiving, trembling, faint-hearted ones. While feeling their own unworthiness, may they remember they go to commemorate the infinite *worthiness* of him who is *Allworthy*. May they hear thy voice of encouragement saying, "Fear not, for I know that ye seek Jesus who was crucified."

Go forth this day everywhere with the preaching of thy holy Gospel. May wanderers be reclaimed; may mourners be comforted; may saints be edified; may thy name be glorified.

We commend to thy paternal keeping our beloved friends. May they be among the number of thy sealed ones. Sanctify them in body, soul, and spirit, that they may at last be presented faultless and unblameable before thy dear Son at his appearing. Bless this household; let us all at last sit down, one united and undivided family, with Abraham, and Isaac, and Jacob, at the better feast of communion in thy heavenly kingdom. And all that we ask is for the sake of Jesus Christ, our crucified, but now risen and exalted Savior. Amen.

EVENING OF A COMMUNION SABBATH.

Most gracious God, who hast in thy good providence brought us to the close of another Sabbath, we entreat thee to accept of our unfeigned thanks for all the loving-kindness and tender mercy thou hast made this day to pass before us. We bless thee for all that our eyes have seen, and ears have heard, of the Word of life. May the benediction and blessing of the Master of the feast rest upon us. May we descend from the holy mount rejoicing in the presence of him who brought us into his own banqueting house, and caused his banner over us to be love. Give us grace to pay the vows which our lips have this day uttered; fulfill in us all the good pleasure of thy goodness, and the work of faith with power, that the name of the Lord Jesus Christ may be magnified. As we have named his precious name anew, may we henceforth depart from all iniquity. Send us help out of thy sanctuary, and strenghten us out of Zion:— may the Lord grant us the desires of our hearts, and fulfill all our petitions. May a Communion Sabbath's services diffuse a hallowed glow over all the duties and engagements of the week:—may we show to the world that we have been with Jesus, and that it has been no vain thing for us to draw near unto God.

Lord, our own strength is weakness; but we will go in the strength of the Lord God. May we be kept by thy mighty power. Let us hear thy monitory voice ever saying to us,—"When thou thinkest thou standest, take heed lest thou fall." Keep us from the beginnings of sin; preserve us from venturing on uncertain ground; may we ever be where we should wish to be found by our Lord when he cometh.

We pray for those who have joined with us this day in the same solemn and sacred ordinance. We commend each and all to the great Shepherd of the sheep, who, through the blood of the everlasting covenant, will make them perfect to do his will.

Regard, in thy great mercy, any who may have been prevented from waiting upon thee in thy house and in thine ordinances. May they that tarry at home divide the spoil. Compensate, by an increased supply of thine own promised grace, for the want of public services. Transform every sick-chamber, and every death-bed, into the house of God and the gate of heaven. May valuable lives be prolonged. May the bereaved be comforted : may they repose on him who *bare* their sorrows and who *knows* their sorrows.

Take the charge of us this night ; watch over us during the unconscious hours of sleep ; may we all come at last to the eternal blessedness of an uninterrupted Communion Sabbath in glory, around which no shadows shall fall ;—for " there shall be no night there, and they need no candle, neither light of the sun, for the Lord God giveth them light, and they shall reign forever and ever." Amen.

FOR A TIME OF BEREAVEMENT.

O Lord God almighty, we rejoice to think that "the Lord reigneth;"—that though thy way sometimes seems to be in the sea, and thy path in the deep waters, and thy judgments unsearchable, yet that nothing can happen by accident or chance—but all is the unerring dictate of infinite wisdom and unchanging faithfulness and love.

Where would we be at this hour, but for the blessed assurance, "*This* also cometh from the Lord of Hosts," who though "wonderful in counsel," is ever "excellent in working." Often we cannot discern, through our tears, the rectitude and love of thy varied dispensations.

Thou didst it. Man may err, and has often erred; but, O unerring God! Thy faithfulness thou hast established in the heavens;—the Judge of all the earth must do right. We would seek to lie submissive at thy feet, and say, "Thy will be done."

Lord, abundantly sanctify this solemn dispensation to every member of our household,—to all our friends and neighbors. May the monitory voice sound loudly in our ears, "Be ye also ready." It is another testimony borne to the truth, that at such a time as we think not, the Son of God may come. May it be ours ever to live in preparation for that solemn event which awaits us all. Whatsoever our hand findeth to do, may we do it with our might, remembering that there is no work, nor device, nor labor, nor repentance in the grave, whither we are going.

Enable us to look forward to that blessed hope and that glorious appearing, when "them also which sleep in Jesus will God bring with him."

Lord, meanwhile descend, and to the friendless prove a Friend. O thou Helper of the helpless, thou Comforter of all that are cast down, thou better and dearer than the dearest and best of earthly relatives, give us that grace which thou hast promised specially in seasons of weakness; may we realise the truth of thy own precious promise, " As thy day is, so shall thy strength be." Deep is now calling to deep, all thy waves and thy billows are going over us; yet the Lord will command his loving-kindness in the day-time, and in the night his song shall be with us, and our prayer to the God of our life. However low we may be sunk under the waves, the arm of thy love and upholding grace are lower still. May it be our sweet experience, that the deeper we sink, we discover more the infinite depths of thy love and mercy. May this thought reconcile us to bear all and suffer all—' we shall soon be done with a present evil world, and be with our God, and that forever and ever.'

Do thou hide us meanwhile in the clefts of the Smitten Rock, until this and all other of earth's calamities be over-past. May we trust thee where we cannot trace thee; and wait patiently for the great day of disclosures, when all shall be revealed, and all be found redounding to the praise and the glory of thy great name.

Hear us, blessed God; and all that we ask is for the sake of thy dear Son, our only Lord and Savior. Amen.

PRAYER TO BE USED BY A FAMILY DETAINED FROM PUBLIC WORSHIP.

Almighty and everlasting God, thou art glorious in holiness, fearful in praises, continually doing wonders. Thy kingdom is an everlasting kingdom, thy dominion endureth throughout all generations. Amid all the changes and vicissitudes of a changing world thou the Lord changest not. Thou art the same, and thy years shall have no end.

We desire to bless and praise thy holy name for the return of another day of the Son of man. This is the day which the Lord hath made, we will rejoice and be glad in it. Do thou go forth everywhere with the preaching of the everlasting gospel. Clothe thy ministers with salvation: let thy saints shout aloud for joy. May the assemblies of thy people be enabled to worship thee in the beauties of holiness, and feel it to be good for them to draw near unto God. It is our comfort to know that thou art not confined to temples made with hands;—that wherever there is a true worshipper, *there*, there is a prayer-hearing God. O thou God of Bethel—God of our fathers, and the covenant God of all who truly fear thee, do thou look down in kindness on us who are prevented this day, by the restraints of thy Providence from joining with our fellow-Christians in the public services of the sanctuary. It is not to numbers thou lookest:—wherever two or three are gathered together in thy name, we have thine own recorded promise, that there thou wilt be in the midst of them to bless them and to do them good. Though thou lovest the gates of Zion, thou art not confined to temples made with hands.

Let the pillar of thy promised presence go before us; may we feel like thy disciples of old, when the voices of heavenly messengers on the mount were silenced—that we are "alone with Jesus." Gracious Savior, abide thou with us; we are independent of all ordinances if we have thee. It is thy presence and love which gives a blessing to all outward means of grace; thy most hallowed altar is the altar of a humble, lowly, contrite heart; thy most acceptable sacrifice is the incense of grateful love—of devoted, obedient, submissive lives.

Lord, may every returning Sabbath be finding us better prepared for the eternal Sabbath. May sin be dying within us. May we be progressively advancing in the divine life. May we be abounding in faith, and hope, and love; seeking by thy grace to walk in newness of life—more humbly—more consistently, more prayerfully. May we live as dying creatures. May all the selemn events that are taking place among ourselves and around us, be so many voices proclaiming, "Arise and depart ye, for this is not your rest."

Do thou look down in mercy on all our dear friends; may they too see the good of thy chosen, and glory with thine inheritance; may the fragrance of this day's services follow them throughout the week; may they have the increasing experience that the way of holiness is the way of happiness.

And now, Lord, what wait we for? Our hope for ourselves, and for all near and dear to us, is in thee. Hear us for the sake of him whom thou hearest always, and in whose most precious name and words we would further pray, saying, Our Father, etc.

PRAYER TO BE USED AT THE BEDSIDE OF A DYING BELIEVER.

Ever Blessed God, we rejoice to know that our times are in thy hands. The Lord gives us our lives—the Lord has a sovereign right to take them away; give us grace to say, "Blessed be the name of the Lord!" Do thou look down in great mercy on thy servant, whom thou art about to take to thyself. Let him know, that, leaning on Jesus, the sting is plucked away from death, and the grave is robbed of its victory. Oh, thou ever-living Redeemer, thou great "Abolisher of Death," who hast brought life and immortality to light by the Gospel, smooth this dying pillow —let thy voice be heard, saying, "Fear not, it is I; be not afraid!" Grant relief from suffering. Give him a peaceful entrance into glory: may thine angels even now be waiting to waft him to thy presence—may he know that thou art faithful who hast promised, "Lo, I am with you alway, even unto the end of the world!" Forgive, oh, forgive all his past sins. May this be the one glorious truth to which his soul clings in a dying hour: "The blood of Jesus Christ, God's Son, cleanseth from all sin." Lord, may thine own blessed soul-sustaining peace be his; a few more moments and he will wake up in heaven; sorrow and sighing shall have fled away forever. May he feel that to depart and to be with Christ is indeed far better. Hear us, good Lord, for Jesus' sake. Amen.

"And I heard a voice from heaven saying unto me, Write, Blessed are the dead which die in the Lord from henceforth: Yea, saith the Spirit, that they may rest from their labors; and their works do follow them."

"In my Father's house there are many mansions; if it were not so, I would have told you. I go to prepare a place for you; and if I go to prepare a place for you, I will come again and receive you unto myself, that where I am there ye may be also."

"When thou passest through the waters I will be with thee; and through the rivers, they shall not overflow thee: when thou walkest through the fire, thou shalt not be burnt; neither shall the flame kindle upon thee. For I am the Lord thy God, the Holy One of Israel, thy Savior."

"Yea, though I walk through the valley of the shadow of death, I will fear no evil, for thou art with me, thy rod and thy staff they comfort me."

"For we know that if our earthly house of this tabernacle were dissolved, we have a building of God, an house not made with hands, eternal in the heavens."

"And one of the elders answered, saying unto me, What are these which are arrayed in white robes? and whence came they? And I said unto him, Sir, thou knowest. And he said unto me, These are they which came out of great tribulation, and have washed their robes, and made them white in the blood of the Lamb. Therefore are they before the throne of God, and serve him day and night in his temple; and he that sitteth on the throne shall dwell among them. They shall hunger no more, neither thirst any more; neither shall the sun light on them, nor any heat. For the Lamb which is in the midst of the throne shall feed them, and shall lead them unto living fountains of waters; and God shall wipe away all tears from their eyes." Amen.

A PRAYER TO BE UTTERED BY THE SICK.

FROM JEREMY TAYLOR'S "HOLY LIVING."

O holy Jesus, thou art a merciful High-priest, and touched with the sense of our infirmities; thou knowest the sharpness of my sickness and the weakness of my person. The clouds are gathered about me, and thou hast covered me with thy storm: my understanding hath not such apprehension of things as formerly. Lord, let thy mercy support me, thy Spirit guide me, and lead me through the valley of this death safely; that I may pass it patiently, holily, with perfect resignation; and let me rejoice in the Lord, in the hopes of pardon, in the expectation of glory, in the sense of thy mercies, in the refreshments of thy Spirit, in a victory over all temptations.

Thou hast promised to be with us in tribulation: Lord, my soul is troubled, and my body is weak, and my hope is in thee, and my enemies are busy and mighty; now make good thy holy promise. Now, O holy Jesus, now let thy hand of grace be upon me: restrain my spiritual enemies, and give me all sorts of spiritual assistances. Lord, remember thy servant in the day when thou bindest up thy jewels.

O take from me all tediousness of spirit, all impatience and unquietness: let me possess my soul in patience, and resign my soul and body into thy hands, as into the hands of a faithful Creator, and a blessed Redeemer. Amen.

A PRAYER OF PARENTS FOR THEIR CHILDREN.

O Lord our God, the God of the spirits of all flesh! all souls are thine, the souls of the parents and the souls of the children are thine, and thou hast grace sufficient for both.

Thou wast our fathers' God, and as such we will exalt thee; thou art our children's God, and also we will plead with thee, for the promise is to us and to our children, and thou art a God in covenant with believers and their seed.

Lord, it is thy good providence that hath built us up into a family. We thank thee for the children thou hast graciously given thy servants; the Lord that hath blessed us with them, make them blessings indeed to us, that we may never be tempted to wish we had been written childless.

We lament the iniquity which our children are conceived and born in; and that corrupt nature which they derive through our loins.

But we bless thee there is a fountain opened for their cleansing from that original pollution, and that they were betimes by baptism dedicated to thee, and admitted into the bonds, and under the blessings of thy covenant; that they are born in thy house, and taken in as members of thy family upon earth.

It is a comfort to us to think that they are baptized, and we desire humbly to plead it with thee; they are thine, save them; enable them, as they become capable, to make it their own act and deed to join themselves unto the Lord, that they may be owned as thine in that day when thou makest up thy jewels.

Give them a good capacity of mind, and a good disposition, make them submissive and tractable, and willing
to receive instruction; incline them betimes to religion and
virtue: Lord, give them wisdom and understanding, and
drive out the foolishness that is bound up in their hearts.

Save them from the vanity which childhood and youth
are subject to, and fit them every way to live comfortably
and usefully in this world. We ask not for great things in
this world for them : give them if it please thee, a strong
and healthful constitution of body, preserve them from all
accidents, and feed them with food convenient for them,
occording to their rank.

But the chief thing we ask of God for them is, that
thou wilt pour thy Spirit upon our seed, even thy blessing,
that blessing of blessings, upon our offspring, that they
may be a seed to serve thee, which shall be accounted
unto the Lord for a generation. Give them that good part
which shall never be taken away from them.

Give us wisdom and grace to bring them up in thy
fear, in the nurture and admonition of the Lord, with meekness and tenderness, and having them in subjection with all
gravity. Teach us how to teach them the things of God
as they are able to bear them, and how to reprove and
admonish, and when there is need to correct them in a
right manner; and how to set them good examples of
everything that is virtuous and praise-worthy, that we may
recommend religion to them, and so train them up in the
way wherein they should go, that if they live to be old,
they may not depart from it.

Keep them from the snare of evil company, and all the
temptations to which they are exposed, and make them
betimes sensible how much it is their interest, as well as
their duty, to be religious : and, Lord, grant that none that

come of us, may come short of eternal life, or be found on the left hand of Christ in the great day.

We earnestly pray that Christ may be formed in their souls betimes, and that the seeds of grace may be sown in their hearts while they are young; and we may have the satisfaction of seeing them walking in the truth, and setting their faces heavenwards. Give them now to hear counsel and receive instruction, that they may be wise in their latter end : and if they be wise, our hearts shall rejoice, even ours.

Prosper the means of their education ; let our children be taught of the Lord, that great may be their peace; and give them so to know thee, the only true God, and Jesus Christ whom thou hast sent, as may be life eternal to them.

O that they may betimes get wisdom, and get understanding, and never forget it : as far as they are taught the truth as it is in Jesus, give them to continue in the things which they have learned.

It is our heart's desire and prayer that our children may be praising God on earth, when we are gone to praise him in heaven, and that we and they may be together forever, serving him day and night in his temple.

If it should please God to remove any of them from us while they are young, let us have grace submissively to resign them to thee, and let us have hope in their death.

If thou remove us from them while they are young, be thou thyself a Father to them, to teach them and provide for them, for with thee the fatherless findeth mercy.

Thou knowest our care concerning them, we cast it upon thee ; ourselves and ours we commit to thee.

Let not the light of our family religion be put out with us, nor that treasure be buried in our graves, but let those that come after us do thee more and better service in their day than we have done in ours, and be unto thee for a name and a praise.

In these prayers we aim at thy glory. Father, let thy name be sanctified in our family; there let thy kingdom come, and let thy will be done by us and ours, as it is done by the angels in heaven; for Christ Jesus' sake, our blessed Savior and Redeemer, whose seed shall endure forever, and his throne as the days of heaven. Now to the Father, Son, and Holy Ghost, that great and sacred name, into which we and our children were baptized, be honor and glory, dominion and praise, henceforth and forever. Amen.

A PRAYER TO BE USED BY CHILDREN.

O God, thou art my God, early will I seek thee. Thou art my God, and I will praise thee; my father's God, and I will extol thee.

Who is a God like unto thee, glorious in holiness, fearful in praises, doing wonders?

Whom have I in heaven but thee? and there is none upon earth that I desire besides thee. When my flesh and my heart fail, thou art the strength of my heart and my portion forever.

Thou madest me for thyself, to show forth thy praise. God be merciful to me a sinner.

O deliver me from the wrath to come, through Christ Jesus, who died for me, and rose again.

Lord, give me a new nature. Let Jesus Christ be formed in my soul, that to me to live may be Christ, and to die may be gain.

Lord, I was in my baptism given up to thee; receive me graciously, and love me freely.

Lord Jesus, thou hast encouraged little children to come to thee, and hast said, that of such is the kingdom of God; I come to thee; O make me a faithful subject of thy kingdom, take me up in thy arms, put thy hands upon me, and bless me.

O give me grace to redeem me from all iniquity, and particularly from the vanity which childhood and youth are subject to.

Lord, give me a wise and understanding heart, that I may know and do thy will in everything, and may in nothing sin against thee.

Lord, grant that from my childhood I may know the Holy Scriptures, and may continue in the good things that I have learned.

Remove from me the way of lying, and grant me thy law graciously.

Lord, be thou a Father to me; teach me and guide me; provide for me, and protect me, and bless me, even me, O my Father.

Bless all my relations, (father, mother, brothers, sisters,) and give me grace to do my duty to them in everything.

Lord, prepare me for death, and give me wisely to consider my latter end.

O Lord, I thank thee for all thy mercies to me; for life and health, food and raiment, and for my education; for my creation, preservation, and all the blessings of this life; but above all, for thine inestimable love in the redemption of the world by our Lord Jesus Christ, for the means of grace, and the hope of glory.

Thanks be to God for his unspeakable gift; blessed be God for Jesus Christ. None but Christ, none but Christ for me.

Now to God the Father, the Son, and the Holy Ghost, that great name into which I was baptized, be honor and glory, dominion and praise, forever and ever. Amen.

Our Father, which art in heaven, etc.

ANOTHER PRAYER FOR CHILDREN.

WRITTEN IN THE YEAR 1703 BY REV. MATTHEW HENRY.

O Lord, thou art an infinite and eternal Spirit, most wise and powerful, holy, just and good.

Thou art the great God who madest the world, and art my Creator; and thou who madest me dost preserve and maintain me, and in thee I live and move, and have my being. O that I may remember thee as my Creator in the days of my youth, and never forget thee.

Lord, give me grace to serve and honor thee, to worship and obey thee, and in all my ways to trust in thee, and to please thee.

Lord, I thank thee for thy holy word, which thou hast given me to be the rule of my faith and obedience, and which is able to make me wise unto salvation.

I confess, O Lord, that the condition which I was born in is sinful and miserable. I am naturally prone to that which is evil, and backward to that which is good, and foolishness is bound up in my heart, and I am by nature a child of wrath; so that if thou hadst not raised up a Savior for me, I had been certainly lost and undone forever.

But, blessed, and forever blessed be God for the Savior Jesus Christ, the eternal Son of God, and the only Mediator between God and man, who took our nature upon him, and became man, that he might redeem and save us.

Lord, I bless thee, for his holy life, give me to follow his steps; I bless thee for the true and excellent doctrines which he preached, help me to receive them in faith. I bless thee for the miracles which he wrought to confirm his doctrine; and especially that he died the cursed death of the cross to satisfy for sin, and to reconcile us to God; and that he rose again from the dead on the third day, and ascended up into heaven, where he ever lives, making intercession for us, and hath all power both in heaven and in earth; and that we are assured he will come again in glory to judge the world at the last day.

Lord, I thank thee that I am one of his disciples; for I am a baptized Christian; and I give glory to Father, Son, and Holy Ghost, in whose name I was baptized.

Lord, be thou in Christ to me a God, and make me one of thy people.

Be thou my chief good and highest end; let Jesus Christ be my prince and Savior; and let the Holy Ghost be my sanctifier, teacher, guide, and comforter.

Lord, enable me to deny all ungodliness, and worldly fleshly lusts, and live soberly, righteously, and goldly, in this present world, always looking for the blessed hope.

Work in me repentance towards God, and faith towards our Lord Jesus Christ; and give me to live a life of faith and repentance.

Lord, make me truly sorry in what I have offended thee, in what I have thought, and spoken, and done amiss, and give me grace to sin no more.

And enable me to receive Jesus Christ, and to rely upon him as my prophet, priest and king, and to give up myself to be ruled and taught, and saved by him.

Lord, grant unto me the pardon of my sins, the gift of the Holy Ghost, and eternal life.

And give me grace to manifest the sincerity of my faith and repentance, by a diligent and conscientious obedience to all thy commandments.

Enable me to love thee with all my heart, and to love my neighbor as myself.

Give me grace always to make mention of thy name with reverence and seriousness, to read and hear thy word with diligence and attention, to meditate upon it, to believe it, and to frame my life according to it.

Lord, grant that I may receive all thy mercies with thankfulness, and bear all afflictions with patience, and submission to thy holy will.

Lord, grant that my heart may never be lifted up with pride, disturbed with anger, or any sinful passion; and that my body may never be defiled with intemperance, uncleanness, or any fleshly lusts; and keep me from ever speaking any sinful words.

Lord give me grace to reverence and obey my parents and governors; I thank thee for their instructions and reproofs; I pray thee bless them to me, and make me in everything a comfort to them.

Lord, pity, help, and succor the poor, and those in afflictions and distress.

Lord, bless my friends, forgive my enemies, and enable me to do my duty to all men.

Wherein I have in anything affended thee, I humbly pray for pardon in the blood of Christ, and grace to do my duty better for the time to come, and so to live in the fear of God, as that I may be happy in this world, and that to come.

Lord, prepare me to die, and leave this world: O save me from that state of everlasting misery and torment, which will certainly be the portion of all the wicked and ungodly, and bring me safe to the world of everlasting rest and joy with thee and Jesus Christ.

And give me wisdom and grace to live a holy, godly life, and to make it my great care and business to serve thee, and to save my own soul.

All this I humbly beg in the name, and for the sake of Jesus Christ, my blessed Savior and Redeemer, to whom with thee, O Father, and the eternal Spirit, be honor, glory, and praise, henceforth and for evermore. Amen.

PRAYERS FOR OPENING A SUNDAY-SCHOOL.

Almighty God, our heavenly Father, we thank thee for thy mercy which thou hast manifested unto us, in watching over and preserving us during another week, in providing for all our wants, and in bringing us together again in this place of instruction. We beseech thee to fill our hearts with sincere love to thy Holy Word, that we may learn to know thee more perfectly as thou art, and Jesus Christ whom thou hast sent into the world to redeem us from all our sins. We pray thee to grant that we and all mankind may believe in him, and love, serve and obey him unto everlasting life.

We thank thee for the precious promises of thy Word and for the hopes of the gospel. We thank thee that we enjoy so many privileges of learning thy will, and that thy truth is so plain that very little children may understand the things which are pleasing to thee and good for us. Oh, help every one of us—both scholars and teachers—to learn thy will with more delight. Give us thy Spirit, to fill us with love to thee and thy commandments.

Gracious Redeemer, grant wisdom to the teachers of this school, to enable them to teach thy truth with plainness. Make their hearts deeply anxious for the spiritual welfare of their respective classes. Give the children understanding and obedient hearts. Cause this school, which is dear to us, and which we believe is dear to thee, to be a means of everlasting good to all who belong to it. Do thou draw the hearts of the children to thy church, and may they all become active in thy kingdom. Oh, may they grow up to be unto thee a peculiar people, zealous of good works.

Give us true repentance for our sins, and blot them out of thy book. Ever keep us in thy fear as long as we remain on the earth, and then raise us to the glory of heaven: and we will give all the praise of our salvation to the Father, the Son and the Holy Ghost. Amen.

Our Father, who art in heaven, look in tender compassion on us, thy dependent children, as we are assembled before thee. We thank thee for preserving our life and health during the past week, and bringing us hither on this thy holy day to be instructed in the truths of thy Word. Our blessed Savior has told us that thou art more willing to grant us thy Holy Spirit than earthly parents are to give good gifts to their children. Pour out his sacred influences, therefore, upon us at this time, that these children may be attentive to the instructions of their teachers, and that we all, both teachers and pupils, may take to heart the truths of thy Holy Word. Fill us with love to thee, and to Jesus Christ thy Son our Savior. May we all be punctual in our attendance at school, and endeavor to discharge our duties in a reverent and devout manner. Teach these children to love the Sabbath and its privileges. Bless our dear pastor and teachers, who labor for the good of souls from Sabbath to Sabbath. Enable us to be faithful in training these children to be useful members of thy church on earth, and preparing them for entrance into thy heavenly kingdom, there to dwell forever with the blessed Savior and his holy angels, and with all who love the Lord Jesus: and we will ascribe all the praise and glory to God the Father, the Son and Holy Spirit. Amen.

Our Father, who art in heaven, we desire to come before thee in deep humility of soul. We adore thee for thy greatness and glory. We worship thee as the Maker and Governor of all things. We praise thee as the Giver and Preserver of our lives. Help us with sincere hearts to thank thee for all thy goodness toward us, in providing for all our wants, in continuing to us health, and friends, and home, and all the comforts of life we enjoy. Make us all deeply thankful to thee for all thy mercy towards us in granting us the gift of a Savior and all the instructions of thy Word. We thank thee for thy church, which thou hast planted in the world, for the holy Sabbathday, and all the other blessings and privileges which thou hast graciously given us. We also thank thee for the Sabbath-school, in which so many of the children and youths of this day are taught to know and fear thee.

O Lord, thou unspeakably great and adorable One, draw nigh to us all at this time. Let thy Holy Spirit more deeply impress our hearts with a sense of our sinfulness. We confess that we have greatly offended thee by breaking thy Holy Commandments. We have often sinned by thought and word and deed. Help us truly to sorrow over our forgetfulness of thy will, and to hate all sin with perfect hatred. Help all of us, even to the least among us, to trust in our blessed Savior, Jesus Christ. Do thou, most merciful God, for his sake forgive all our sins. Fill our hearts with love to thee and with reverence for thy Holy Laws. Take away from us all evil tempers and desires, and help us every day to become more like our blessed Savior, who never did any sin, but was always gentle and harmless. Help all these children to love and keep holy the Sabbath day, and to delight in the Sabbath-school and the church. May their hearts find great pleasure in thy Holy Bible, which is the best of all books. May they love to sing thy praises and to pray to thee for thy favor every day.

O Lord, we pray for thy blessing to descend on all the

families to which we belong. Make all the parents of these children pious and kind. Oh, may all the scholars in this school have good instructions and examples given them at home, and may their homes be very happy. Bless the teachers of this Sabbath-school. May they love the work of teaching the young more than ever. Help them to consider the greatness of the work given them to do ; and may they do it with zeal. Assist the pupils all to delight in the instructions of their teachers, and to profit by the same. Oh, may they love thee, their parents and friends, their brothers and sisters, their schoolmates, and all mankind. May much good be done here in thy name this day. May we all love and follow the Savior as long as we live in the world, and when we die, be raised to the joys and glories of heaven. Grant these, and all other blessings we need, for the sake of our blessed and only Savior. Amen.

O Lord, our most merciful Redeemer, who didst take up little children in thine arms, and didst bless them, look down graciously on us and bless us also. We confess that we are sinners; from the youngest to the eldest of us, we have erred and strayed from thee like lost sheep. But, O Lord, have mercy on us; turn us, and so shall we be turned; and wash away all our guilt in the blood of Jesus Christ, our only Mediator and Advocate. O thou, who out of the mouths of babes and sucklings hast ordained praise, fill our hearts, we beseech thee, with love, and our lips with thanksgiving. To thy goodness we owe every blessing we enjoy. While other children are suffering hunger and disease and cold, thou art doing us good by day and by night, and giving us food, and health, and raiment. We bless thee for these thy mercies towards us; but, above all, we bless thee for the redeeming love of Christ, for all the means of grace, and for the hope of glory. O God, the Creator and Preserver of all mankind, we beseech thee for all sorts and conditions of men. Bless the country and all the officers of government; bless thy church, and give her speedy victory over all her enemies; bless all Sunday-schools, with their officers and teachers, and make them more and more useful. Let thy blessing descend also upon the ministers of the gospel; and may thy kingdom be established in the hearts of all people. Look down in mercy on our relations and friends, and teach them to value thy favor above life itself. Finally, we beseech thee to bless us, even us also; help us to improve the hours we spend within these walls; as scholars, make us obedient to our teachers and kind to our companions.

Especially bless us on this holy day. May thy presence dwell with us in thy house of prayer, enable us to worship thee in spirit and in truth, and prevent us from being drowsy or forgetful hearers of thy word.

Open our understandings to understand the Holy Scriptures. Endue our souls with every holy disposition, and preserve us from the corruptions and evils which are in the world. We ask every blessing for the sake of Jesus Christ, our Savior. Amen.

Almighty and most merciful God, who hast graciously promised in thy Holy Word to hear the united prayers of thy children, we humbly beseech thee to accept the offering of our thanks for the preservation of our lives, our powers and faculties, and all our outward comforts and advantages. Help us now to read thy Word, and to receive instruction in the doctrines of salvation with attention and meekness, that our souls may be nourished with bread from heaven, and that we may be made meet to live with thee and Jesus Christ our Savior forever and ever.

. Help all of us to feel more deeply how sinful and help-less we are. Lead us all to be truly humble before thee, because of our unworthiness. Give grace to both teachers and pupils to be sincerely sorry for all the sins we have ever committed against thee ; and do thou in much mercy forgive us all the evil we have ever done. Grant us thy grace, that we may hereafter watch and pray, lest we enter into temptation.

Bless this Sabbath-school in all its members and rela-tions. Make it a means of great good to all this neighbor-hood. May the children and youth who here learn thy will, grow up in thy fear and be found walking in the ways of piety. May they be obedient to their parents, attentive to their teachers, and kind to each other. Bless also the families which are here represented.

Let thy blessing, merciful Father, be given to Sabbath-schools everywhere. Make them more and more useful to the church of our blessed Redeemer. Let thy kingdom of grace and peace extend 'throughout the world, that the name of our God—Father, Son and Holy Spirit—may be glorified throughout the world and forever. Amen.

Holy and merciful God, we praise and adore thee as the giver of life and all our blessings. We do thank thee that though thou art so great that the angels cannot tell thy greatness, yet thou dost think of us and all our wants. We thank thee that though thou hast never had a begin-ning, and wilt forever continue to exist, thou dost remember us weak and dying creatures.

We are again before thee as a Sabbath-school, because thou didst in mercy watch over us through another week. We confess that we have not deserved thy goodness towards us, because we have been forgetful of thee, and have

broken thy Holy Commandments. Help us all, both teach-·
ers and scholars, to unite in worshiping thee in spirit and in
truth. While we appear before thee with our lips, may
our hearts be not far from thee. O Lord, help us always
sincerely to desire what we ask of thee with our words.
May all our singing, all our praying, and all our teaching
and learning, be acceptable before thee.

O Lord, give us thy Holy Spirit to fill us with love to
thee and all that is good. May he help us to understand
thy holy will, and to take great delight in obeying thee.
Assist us to engage in the lessons of the school this day
with attentive and solemn minds. May all things be done
decently and in order. May all the teachers remember that
it is a great work to teach even a little child the way to the
Savior and to heaven. Do thou in mercy incline all the
pupils of this school to lay up in their minds all the good
things they here learn from the Bible. While the children
are taught the meaning and the holiness of thy commandments, and the wickedness of sin, lead them to see and feel
how greatly they have sinned against thee, the greatest and
best of all beings. May they all sorrow over their sins and
lament that they are sinners, so that they may believe in
Jesus Christ, the Savior of men. Oh, fill their souls with
love to the Savior, that they may ever follow him. Help
them to be Christian children, so that if they should soon
be taken away by death, they may be prepared for heaven;
or, that if they should live to become men and women, they
may be very faithful members of thy church, and be greatly
useful in thy service.

We thank thee that in thy providence thou hast
raised up the institution of the Sabbath-school. Grant thy
blessing upon Sabbath-schools wherever they are held.
May they become more useful than they have ever been;

and do thou cause them to spread throughout the whole world.

And now, O our Father and God, we pray thee to pardon all our sins. May our hearts and our lives become more and more pure. Help us to overcome all temptations and to avoid all sinful company. Give us grace to love and praise thee as long as we live. And whatever else thou seest we need to make us blessed in this world and the next, be thou pleased in mercy to give us, through our Lord Jesus Christ. Amen.

PRAYERS FOR CLOSING A SUNDAY-SCHOOL.

O God, our heavenly Father, before we close these exercises, we would give thanks unto thee for all things which we have received from thy bountiful Providence. Grant, we pray thee, that all that we have heard at this time may be blessed to the enlightening of our understanding and to the sanctification of our hearts, that the power of thy word may appear in our whole life. Preserve us, O Lord of mercy, from all folly and temptation by which our hearts way be corrupted, the seed of thy word destroyed, and our souls polluted. Let thy good Spirit always dwell within us, and create in us a pure heart, and lead us in the way everlasting. Guard us from all dangers, and protect us from all evil, during the week which we have now commenced; and, if it be thy will, bring us together again, to praise thee with purer hearts for thy mercy and goodness.

Most merciful Father, may it please thee to bless these thy servants, who labor to impart unto these dear children a true knowledge of thee and of the way of salvation through our Lord Jesus Christ. Enlighten them by thy Word and Spirit; encourage and strengthen them in all their endeavors to serve thee, and make them instrumental in leading many of these precious young souls into thy kingdom of grace and happiness; and help them at all times so to attend to the instructions and admonitions of their teachers, that they may have joy in them. And as they can never recompense them for their labors of love in their behalf, we beseech thee to follow them all the days of their lives with thy goodness, and to bring us and them to the enjoyment of eternal life, through Jesus Christ our Lord, to whom,

with thee and the Holy Ghost, be honor and glory forever
and ever. Amen.

———————————

Almighty and ever blessed God, at the close of this
hour's instructions, we again present ourselves before thee
to offer our humble prayer at thy throne. We come in the
name of that Savior who graciously said, Suffer little children to come unto me, and forbid them not, for of such is
the kingdom of heaven. We thank thee that we have been
permitted, as teachers and pupils, to spend a happy hour
together in singing thy praise and attending to the precious
truths of thy Word. Teach us all to feel that by nature
and practice we are sinners in a state of condemnation; that
we must be converted and become new creatures in Christ
Jesus, if we would enter into the kingdom of heaven. Enable us to examine our hearts and life, to learn whether we
have experienced this great change. Assist us to inquire
whether we are thy children indeed; whether we love thee,
our God and Savior, supremely, and our fellow-men as ourselves, and whether we make thy service the business of
our life. Preserve us from the follies of youth and from the
temptations of the world, and bring us together again to
spend many happy Sabbath hours in thy service. Watch
over us with thy kind providence in the house and by the
way, and wheresoever we may be; teach us to remember
that thou art with us, beholding all we do. Bless our dear
parents, and brothers, and sisters; bless our pastor, and
teachers, and schoolmates; bless all mankind, and especially
thy dear church, embracing all in every land who love the
Lord Jesus Christ, in whose precious words we address
thee. Amen.

———————————

O Lord, whose tender mercies are over us at all times,
we praise and adore thee. We desire ever to remember

that thou hast made us and that we are in thy hands.   As thou hast again granted us the privileges of the Sabbath-school, we would express our thankfulness to thee.   We thank thee for the holy truths of thy Word, on which our minds have been led to think.   We rejoice in the declaration that " God so loved the world, that he gave his only-begotten Son, that whosoever believeth in him should not perish, but have everlasting life."   We thank thee that thy truth, which is made known to the world, is so plain that even little children may understand much of thy will.   We thank thee, O our Savior, that when thou wast on earth as a man, thou didst show thy love to the young, and didst say, " Suffer little children to come unto me."   Do thou kindly draw the precious young hearts of this school to know and fear thee.

Holy and merciful God, follow with thy blessing the truth which has this day been presented to the minds of the classes in this school.   May the labors and prayers of the teachers be acceptable to thee.   Let the minds of all the pupils, even those of little children, retain the good lessons they have this day learned.   May the blessed truths of thy holy religion ever interest and delight their hearts.   May they never be among those persons who know thy will, but do it not.

We pray that these children may all be converted to thee.   May the angels in heaven rejoice over each soul when coming in penitence to its God.   Turn thou the hearts of all from sin to thyself.   May those hearts not be hardened with evil.   Oh, may they be thine now in their tender years, and thine all their days upon the earth.   May the highest hopes of their teachers concerning them be realized.

We unite in sincere prayer for thy Spirit to lead us into all truth.   Whatever is necessary for us to know, may he teach us. Whatever of thy will we have already learned, may he help every one to love and obey. Keep, O Lord, every member of this school from the paths of sin during the coming week. Do thou mercifully guard them from the power of the tempter, who would destroy them. Preserve them from the evils of sinful company, and from the examples of the wicked around them. Bless all the families to which we belong. May much good be carried home to every house. We pray for thy blessing upon all our friends and the whole world. Oh, let the time soon come when all the poor heathen shall be blessed with the gospel.

Guide and keep us through the week that is before us; and, if it be thy will, may we meet again in this happy place when the Sabbath-day returns. Help us to live a holy life here in this world, and make us fully prepared for the happiness and glory of heaven. Hear us in mercy, for the sake of Christ our Redeemer. Amen.

Almighty God, our heavenly Father! Thou hast again blessed us and made us partakers of thy Holy Word. Accept, we beseech thee, our hearty thanks for the great benefits and the inestimable blessings which we enjoy in knowing the Holy Scriptures from our youth, which are able to make us wise unto salvation. Sanctify our souls and enlightenen our understanding, O thou Spirit of the Lord, that the instruction which we have this day received may improve our souls, and make us wise, and happy. Preserve us, we pray thee, from all light-mindedness, and keep our hearts in thy fear, that the allurements of sin and of vice may not mislead nor harm us. Help us to spend the rest of this day in thy fear and love, that we may be strengthened and prepared to serve thee during the week on which we have entered. Enable us to live in the hope of a glorious day of rest hereafter, of a Sabbath in heaven which shall never end, where we shall know thee more perfectly, worship thee in a more spiritual manner, and praise thee with purer affections. Grant that every holy day which we spend on earth may prepare us more and more to enter into thy kingdom of immortality and glory which thou hast promised unto us in Jesus Christ our Lord.

Heavenly Father, enable us, we beseech thee, to render unto our parents due honor and obedience, affection and gratitude. Assist us to submit with pleasure to their friendly guidance, to be patient under reproof, to abhor falsehood, to discharge all our obligations with a dutiful heart, and never to cause them tears and grief by any perverseness. Be pleased, O God, to prolong their health and life, to uphold them by thy gracious providence, to make them happy in us and in all who belong to their family. Let thy goodness follow them continually here, and reward them with eternal happiness beyond the grave, through Jesus Christ thy dear Son our Lord. Amen.

Thou, Lord, who art unspeakably great and merciful, we praise thee for thy goodness and glory. Help us to say from our hearts, Oh, give thanks unto the Lord, for he is good: for his mercy endureth forever. We again worship thy holy name, after a season spent in learning thy will. May we receive grace to cast ourselves very humbly before thy footstool of mercy; and do thou notice and supply our wants.

Do thou graciously help all the children of this school to remember the truth they have this day read and heard. Let the Holy Spirit make deep impressions upon every mind. Lead all to think of their sins against thee, and to look to the only hope which the Savior has made known.

Awaken in each young heart love to the Redeemer of perishing souls. Oh, may that Savior who gave his life for us all, receive the affections and the service of every one present.

Keep these pupils from the wickedness of sin during the week. Help them to be wise with a heavenly wisdom, to shun evil and to follow good. Preserve them from bad company, and help them to delight in virtue and piety. Prepare their hearts for much happiness and usefulness in the divine service. While they enjoy the light of thy holy religion, may they strive to do good to the poor, to the sick, the wicked, the ignorant and the benighted.

May Sabbath-schools extend everywhere throughout our land and all lands. Cause their happy influence to be felt among all nations, and make them far more useful than they have ever been in bringing on the day when the whole world shall be filled with the knowledge of the Lord.

Grant us, O Lord, the forgiveness of all our sins; and when we separate to-day, dismiss us with thy blessing. Lead us in thy holy fear until our days on earth shall close, and then admit us to the perfect joys of heaven, through Jesus Christ our Savior. And to the Father, the Son and the Holy Spirit we will ascribe all the praise and the glory forever. Amen.

Ever-gracious and adorable God, we again call upon thy nane. Another sacred hour of giving and receiving holy instruction is past; and now we look to thee for thy blessing to follow. We thank thee for the privilege of praying unto thee, and that thy Holy Bible contains so many exceedingly great and precious promises to all who seek thee aright.

Mercifully grant thy Spirit to every heart before thee,

that the truth we have learned may do us great good. Take away the stony heart, and give a heart that can feel. Subdue the stubborn will, and bestow a will to agree with thine. Remove the love of sin from every soul, and awaken instead sincere love to thee and thy commandments. Bestow thy blessing richly upon this Sabbath-school. Bless it in all its scholars and teachers, and in all its interests. May thy people ever love it and sustain it, and thy favor ever prosper it. Make it a means of much religious instruction and a nursery of piety. May all the officers and teachers of this school have much grace in their hearts, and do thou help them to show a Christian example to their respective classes. Draw the minds and hearts of all the pupils to thyself. Help them to obey the command, " Remember now thy Creator in the days of thy youth." May none of the children of this school be unmindful of the lessons here received. May they never forget that we must all die, and that if we love not our Savior we cannot go to heaven.

Kind and gracious God and Savior, draw the hearts of the children in love to their teachers and their minister. Incline them more than ever to obey their parents and to be kind to one another. May they love all their friends and all mankind. Do thou touch their hearts with pity for the many poor heathen people and children who have not the Bible, and who know nothing of the Savior or of heaven. Incline them to pray, to labor and to give of their money to the missionary cause. May all our hearts feel for the sick, the poor, the orphan, and those in every condition of misery and wretchedness, and to do all we can for their good.

We confess before thee, O our heavenly Father, that we are sinful and unworthy. We have all sinned against thee more than we can tell. We feel that our hearts have been wicked in thy sight. We have had sinful tempers and passions; we have spoken sinful words; we have committed sinful deeds. But we know that if we are sorry for our sins and trust in the Savior, thou wilt forgive. We beseech thee in much mercy to take away our guilt. Help us to overcome every sin, and do thou make our hearts pure. May we no longer do the things we should not do, or leave undone the things we should do.

Dismiss us now, gracious God, with thy blessing: Grant us every mercy we need during the week. Prepare us for all the trials of life. Should it please thee to continue unto us life and health, bring us again safely together, that we may re-unite in the precious exercises of the Sabbath-school. And when these earthly meetings must at last cease, raise our souls to our heavenly home, where we shall be forever with the Lord, and where we shall be like him, because we shall see him as he is. We implore these and all needed blessings, not on account of any worthiness in in ourselves, but alone for the sake of Christ. Amen.

MATTHIAS CLAUDIUS' EXPOSITION OF THE LORD'S PRAYER.

The aboved named distinguished German Christian author has written a classical exposition of the Lord's prayer, in a letter to his friend Andres, which we will try to translate, although it will be difficult to render many of his idiomatic German phrases into good English. This exposition contains, like a good prayer—*few* words, but *many* and *deep* meanings :

" The Lord's Prayer is, once for all, the best prayer, for you know who composed it. But no man on God's earth, can so pray it, as he meant it; we mutilate it only from a distance, one of us more miserably than the other. But that will do no harm, dear Andres, if we only mean it right, (*gut meinen,*) the dear God (*Liebe Gott*) must always do the best for us, and he knows how it ought to be. As you have requested it, I will tell you sincerely, how I use the Lord's prayer. But I think it is only very poorly done, and I would gladly let some one instruct me how to do it better.

See now, when I want to pray, then I think first of my sainted father, who was so good and kind to me, and gave me so willingly what I needed. And then I imagine (*stell mir vor*) that the whole world is my Father's house : and all the people in Europe, Asia, Africa and America, are, in my mind, my brothers and sisters; and God sits in heaven on a golden throne, and stretches his right hand over the sea, to the end of the world, and his left hand is full of blessing and goodness, and the tops of the mountains round about are crowned with glory—then I begin :

Our Father, who art in heaven, hallowed be thy name.

This, already, I do not yet fully understand. It is said that the Jews had some special mysteries about the names of God. I will let this pass (*lasse gut sein,*) and only wish that the idea (*Andenken*) of God, and every trace (*Spur*), by which we can know him, may be above all things great and holy to me and all mankind.

Thy kingdom come.

At this I think about myself, as things go hither and thither within me; now this and now that controls, which causes all kinds of heart aches. And then I think, how good it would be for me, if God would make an end of all strife, and he himself would rule within me!

Thy will be done in earth as it is in heaven.

Here I think of heaven, and the holy angels who joyfully do his will; whom no pain or sorrow afflicts, and who overflow with love and happiness, in which they rejoice, day and night. And then I think, O, if it were also thus on earth!

Give us this day our daily bread.

Every one knows, what "daily bread" means, and that we must eat, as long as we are in the world, and that it also tastes good. Then I think about this. My children also come into my mind: how they enjoy their meals and eagerly reach out for their food. And then I pray, that the dear God (*Liebe Gott*) would give us something to eat.

And forgive us our trespasses as we forgive those who have trespassed against us.

It hurts, when we are injured, and revenge is sweet. Thus it appears also to me, and I feel an inclination in that way. But then the wicked servant (*Schalks knecht*) in the gospel comes up before mine eyes, and my heart sinks, and

I resolve to forgive my fellow-servant, and never say a word about those hundred pennies.

And lead us not into temptation.

Here I think of all kinds of instances, where people under such and such circumstances departed from the good, and fell, and that this might also happen to me.

But deliver us from evil.

Here I think of the temptations to which we are exposed, and that we are so easily led astray, and lured from the right way. But at the same time I also think of all the ills of life, of consumption and old age, trouble with children, gangrene, and delirium, and the thousand kinds of misery and heartaches in the world, which torment and distress the poor people, while none can help. And you will find, dear Andres, that if the tears have not come before, they will certainly come now, and we long so heartily to be delivered, and feel so sad and cast down, as if there were no help at all. But then we must take courage again (*sich Muth machen*), stretch our hands toward heaven, and exclaim triumphantly, *Thine is the kingdom, and the power, and the glory forever. Amen.*"

ANOTHER PARAPHRASE ON THE LORD'S PRAYER.

Our Father in heaven, we come to thee as children to a Father, able and ready to help us.

We beseech thee, let thy name by sanctified; enable us and others to glorify thee in all that whereby thou hast made thyself known, and dispose of all things to thine own glory.

Let thy kingdom come; let Satan's kingdom be destroyed, and let the kingdom of thy grace be advanced; let us and others be brought into it, and kept in it, and let the kingdom of thy glory be hastened.

Let thy will be done on earth as it is done in heaven; make us by thy grace able and willing to know, obey, and submit to thy will in all things, as the angels do in heaven.

Give us this day our daily bread; of thy free gift let us receive a competent portion of the good things of this life, and let us enjoy thy blessing with them.

And forgive us our debts as we forgive our debtors. We pray that for Christ's sake thou wouldst freely pardon all our sins, and that by thy grace thou wouldst enable us from the heart to forgive others.

And lead us not into temptation, but deliver us from evil. Either keep us, O Lord, from being tempted to sin, or support and deliver us when we are tempted.

For thine is the kingdom, the power, and the glory, forever. Lord we take our encouragement in prayer from thyself only, and desire in our prayers to praise thee, ascribing kingdom, power, and glory to thee; and in testimony of our desires and assurance to be heard through Jesus Christ, we say, Amen.—*Shorter Catechism.*

THE LORD'S PRAYER PARAPHRASED.

The following beautiful paraphrase of the Lord's Prayer has been credited to a Frenchman—M. Pierre Bernard; but in the Life of the Rev. William Marsh, D. D., so long known and so highly esteemed in England, it is stated that during a wakeful night Dr. Marsh compos. d it, and that it was written down from his dictation the next morning. Comparing the two versions, the one ascribed to M. Benard is more full; but it may be merely an amplification of that of Dr. Marsh. We give the following compilation from both, as a fitting conclusion to this Exposition of the Lord's prayer :—

Our Father—
> By right of creation,
> By bountiful provision,
> By gracious adoption;

Which art in heaven—
> The throne of thy glory,
> The home of thy children,
> The temple of thy angels;

Hallowed be thy name—
> By the thoughts of our hearts,
> By the words of our lips,
> By the works of our hands.

Thy kingdom come—
> Of providence to defend us,
> Of grace to refine us,
> Of glory to crown us.

Thy will be done in earth, as it is in heaven—
> Towards us without resistance,
> By us without compulsion,
> Universally without exception,
> Eternally without declension.

Give us this day our daily bread—
> Of necessity for our bodies,
> Of eternal life for our souls.

And forgive us our trespasses—
> Against the commands of thy law,
> Against the grace of thy gospel;

As we forgive those that trespass against us—
>By defaming our character,
>By embezzling our property,
>By abusing our person.

And lead us not into temptation, but deliver us from evil!—
>Of overwhelming afflictions,
>Of worldly enticements,
>Of Satan's devices,
>Of error's seductions,
>Of sinful affections.

For thine is the kingdom, and the power, and the glory, forever—
>Thy kingdom governs all,
>Thy power subdues all,
>Thy glory is above all.

Amen—
>As it is in thy purpose,
>So it is in thy promises ;
>So be it in our prayers,
>So it shall be to thy praise.

By this prayer of our Lord—
>The Father bless,
>The Son adore,
>The Spirit praise,
>Forevermore. Amen and Amen.—*Steel.*

A DISSERTATION ON PRAYER.

BY MATTHEW HENRY.

Prayer is a principal branch of religious worship, which we are moved to by the very light of nature, and obliged to, by some of its fundamental laws. Pythagoras' Golden Verses begin with this precept, "whatever men made a God of, they prayed to." "Deliver me, for thou art my God." Isa. xliv. 17. Nay, whatever they prayed to, they made a God of—*Deos qui rogat, ille facit.* It is a piece of respect and homage so exactly consonant to the natural ideas which all men have of God, that it is certain those that "live without prayer, live without God in the world."

Prayer is the solemn and religious offering up of devout acknowledgments and desires to God, or a sincere representation of holy affections, with a design to give unto God the glory due unto his name thereby, and to obtain from him promised favors, and both through the Mediator. Our English word *prayer* is too strait, for that properly signifies petition or request; whereas humble adorations of God, and thanksgivings to him, are as necessary in prayer, as any other part of it. The Greek word is a vow directed to God. The Latin word *votum* is used for prayer. Jorah's mariners with their sacrifices made vows; for prayer is to move and oblige ourselves, not to move or oblige God. Clemens Alexandrinus calls prayer (with an excuse for the boldness of the expression) a "conversing with God." And it is the scope of a long discourse of his there, to show that the believer lives a life of communion with God, and so is praying always; that he studies by his prayers continually to converse with God. Some (saith he) have their stated hours of prayer, but he "prays all his life long." The Scripture describes prayer to be our drawing near to God, lifting up our souls to him, pouring out our hearts before him.

This is the life and soul of prayer; but this soul in the present state must have a body, and that body must be such as becomes the soul, and is suited and adapted to it. Some words there must be, of the mind at least, in which, as in the smoke, this incense must ascend: not that God may understand us, for our thoughts afar off are known to him, but that we may the better understand ourselves.

A golden thread of heart-prayer must run through the web of the whole Christian life; we must be frequently addressing ourselves to God in short and sudden ejaculations, by which we must keep up our communion with him in providences and common actions, as well as in ordinances and religious services. Thus prayer must be *sparsim* (a sprinkling of it) in every duty, and our eyes must be ever towards the Lord.

In mental prayer thoughts are words, and they are the first born of the soul, which are to be consecrated to God. But if, when we pray alone, we see cause for the better fixing of our minds, and exciting of our devotions, to clothe our conceptions with words; if the conceptions be the genuine products of the new nature, one would think words should not be far to seek. *Verbaque prævisam rem non invita sequuntur.* Nay, if the groanings be such as cannot be uttered, he that searcheth the heart knows them to be the mind of the Spirit, and will accept of them, Rom. viii. 26, 27, and answer the voice of our breathing. Lam. iii. 56. Yet through the infirmity of the flesh, and the aptness of our hearts to wander and trifle, it is often necessary that words should go first, and be kept in mind for the directing and exciting of devout actions, and in order thereunto, the assistance here offered I hope will be of some use.

When we join with others in prayer, who are our mouth to God, our minds must attend them, by an intelligent believing concurrence with that which is the sense, and scope, and substance of what they say, and affections working in us suitable thereunto; and this the Scripture directs us to signify, by saying Amen, mentally if not vocally, "at their giving of thanks." 1 Cor. xiv. 16. And as far as our joining with them will permit, we may intermix pious ejaculations of our own with their addresses, provided they be pertinent, that not the least fragment of praying time may be lost.

But he that is the mouth of others in prayer, whether in public or private, and therein useth that freedom of speech, that holy liberty of prayer which is allowed us, (and which we are sure many good Christians have found by experience to be very comfortable and advantageous in this duty,) ought not only to consult the workings of his own heart, but the edification also of those that join with him; and both in matter and words should have an eye to that; and for service in that case I principally design this endeavor.

It is desirable that our prayers should be copious and full. Our burdens, cares, and wants are many, so are our sins and mercies. The promises are numerous and very rich; our God gives liberally, and hath bid us open our mouths wide, and he will fill them, will satisfy them with good things. We are not straitened in him, why then should we be stinted and straitened in our own bosoms! Christ had taught his disciples the Lord's prayer, and yet tells them, John xvi. 24, that hitherto they had asked nothing, *i. e.* nothing in comparison with what they should ask when the Spirit should be poured out, to abide with the church forever; and they should see greater things than these. "Ask, and ye shall receive, that your joy may be full." We are encouraged to be particular in prayer, and in everything to make our requests known to God, as we ought also to be particular in the adoration of the divine perfections, in the confession of our sins, and our thankful acknowledgments of God's mercies.

But since, at the same time, we cannot go over the tenth part of the particulars which are fit to be the matter of prayer, without making the duty burdensome to the flesh, which is weak, even where the spirit is willing (an extreme which ought carefully to be avoided), and without danger of intrenching upon other religious exercises, it will be requisite that what is but briefly touched upon at one time, should be enlarged upon at another time. And herein this storehouse of materials for prayer may be of use to put us in remembrance of our several errands at the throne of grace, that none may be quite forgotten.

And it is requisite to the decent performance of the duty, that some proper method be observed, not only that what is said to be good, but that it be said in its proper place and time; and that we offer not anything to the glorious Majesty of heaven and earth, which is confused, impertinent, and indigested. Care must be taken then more than ever, that we be not "rash with our mouth, nor hasty to utter anything before God," that we say not what comes uppermost, nor use such repetitions as evidence not the fervency, but the barrenness and slightness of our spirits; but that the matters we are dealing with God about being of such vast importance, we observe a decorum in our words, that they be well chosen, well weighed, and well placed.

And as it is good to be methodical in prayer so it is good to be sententious. The Lord's prayer is remarkably so; and David's psalms, and many of Paul's prayers, which we have in his epistles. We must consider that the greatest part of those that join with us in prayer, will be in danger of losing or mistaking the sense, if the period be long, and the parentheses many; and in this as in other things, they that are strong ought to bear the infirmities of the weak. Jacob must lead as the children and flock can follow.

As to the words and expression we use in prayer, though I have here, in my enlargments upon the several heads of prayer, confined myself almost wholly to scripture language, because I would give an instance of the sufficiency of the scripture to furnish us for every good work, yet I am far from thinking but that it is convenient and often necessary to use other expressions in prayer, besides those that are purely scriptural; only I would advise that the sacred dialect be most used, and made familiar to us and others in our dealing about sacred things; that language Christian people are most accustomed to, most affected with and will most readily agree to; and where the scriptures are opened and explained to the people in the ministry of the word, scripture language will be most intelligible, and the sense of it best apprehended. This is "sound speech that cannot be condemned," and those that are able to do it, may do well to enlarge by way of descant or paraphrase upon the scriptures they make use of; still speaking according to that rule, and comparing spiritual things with spiritual, that they may illustrate each other.

It is not to be reckoned a preventing of scripture, but is agreeable to the usage of many divines, especially the Fathers, and I think is warranted by divers quotations in the New Testament out of the Old, to allude to a scripture phrase, and to make use of it by way of accommodation to another sense than what was the first intendment of it, provided it agree with the analogy of faith. As for instance those words, Psa. lxxxvi. 7, " All my springs are in thee," may very fitly be applied to God, though there it appears, by the feminine article in the original, to be meant of Sion, nor has it ever been thought any wrong to the scripture phrase, to pray for the blessings of " the upper springs," though the expression from whence it is borrowed, Judges i. 15, hath no reference at all to what we mean; but by common use every one knows the signification, and many are pleased with the signification of it.

Perhaps those who covet earnestly this excellent gift, and covet to excel in it, may find it of use to them to have such a book as this interleaved, in which to insert such other heads and expressions as they think will be most agreeable to them, and are wanting here. Though I have here recommended a good method for prayer, and that which has been generally approved, yet I am far from thinking we should always tie ourselves to it; that may be varied as well as the expression. Thanksgivings may very aptly be put sometimes before confession or petition, or our intercessions for others before our petitions for ourselves, as in the Lord's prayer. Sometimes one of these parts of prayer may be enlarged upon much more than another; or they may be decently interwoven in some other method.

There are those, I doubt not who, at sometimes, have their hearts so wonderfully elevated and enlarged in prayer, above themselves; at other times, such a fixedness and fulness of thought, such a fervour of pious and devout affections, the product of which is such a fluency and variety of pertinent and moving expressions, and in such a just and natural method, that then to have an eye to such a scheme as this, would be a hindrance to them, and would be likely to cramp and straiten them. If the heart be full of its good matter, it may make "the tongue as the pen of a ready writer." But this is a case that rarely happens, and ordinarily there is need of proposing to ourselves a certain method in prayer, that the service may be performed decently and in order; in which yet one would avoid that which looks too formal. A man may write straight without having his paper ruled.

But after all, the intention and close application of the mind, the lively exercises of faith and love, and the outgoings of holy desire towards God, are so essentially necessary to prayer, that without these in sincerity, the best and most proper language is but a lifeless image. If we had the tongue of men and angels, and have not the heart of humble serious Christians in prayer, we are but as a sounding brass and a tinkling cymbal. It is only the "effectual fervent prayer," the "in-wrought, in-laid" prayer that "avails much." Thus therefore we ought to approve ourselves to God in the integrity of our hearts, whether we pray by, or without a precomposed form.

THE LIMITATIONS OF PRAYER.

" Ask what ye will and it shall be done unto you," is the gracious assurance of Christ. Does it mean that, in the most absolute sense, we may ask whatever may come into the heart, and expect that it will be given ? The interpretation sometimes put upon the promise would lead us to this conclusion, but is that the meaning of Christ ? It cannot be. The promise is limited to the sphere of prayer. That sphere is large enough to embrace all that is needful for human happiness and salvation, and the promise is ample for all legitimate need, but if we seek to enlarge it, we will not only be disappointed, but we will find the very spirit of prayer failing, and the blessings within our reach fleeing from us.

Prayer is limited to the sphere of holiness. An unholy desire cannot be borne to the mercy seat to be presented by the great Intercessor. It is possible for worldly desires to become so mingled with our better aspirations that we do not detect them, but God does, and he withholds the object we seek, or gives it in judgment. He is enthroned in right.

Prayer is limited by the bounds of God's promises to us. There are certain things which he has not promised. It is legitimate to pray for life, but he has not promised that we will never die, and therefore we may not ask it. He has promised us his protection, but not in the violation of his laws. " Cast thyself down," said the tempter to Christ, and appealed to the promise of angelic protection, but the answer was that the promise was not made for such an act : " It is written, Thou shalt not tempt the Lord thy God." It may be necessary sometimes in the performance of duty to expose ourselves to danger, but to do so needlessly and expect the protection of God is to tempt him. The boundary of the promise may not always be clear to us, but there is a boundary, and in our prayer we should recognize the fact, and offer our petition in that spirit.

The spirit in which prayer is offered may place the petitions beyond the range of acceptance. " Ye ask and receive not, because ye ask amiss, that ye may consume it upon your lusts." One may ask for the highest gifts promised, and at the same time bar the door against his petition by the spirit in which he asks, and the object for which he seeks. In the holiest part of our service, we may so mingle the earthly and sinful that the heavenly will be withheld.

And there is always present the limitation of God's infinitely wise and holy purpose. The interpretation sometimes placed upon prayer changes its character and converts it into imperative command. We sometimes hear what is equivalent to saying that God is bound to give what we ask. God does always hear the prayer of faith, but he does not always grant the petition offered, even when offered in the most reverent and devout faith, for the reason that he is supreme and his purpose must stand. Prayer recognizes this; it belongs to the very nature of prayer to seek that which may be graciously given, and therefore also may be as graciously withheld. God's thoughts are higher than our thoughts, and his ways higher than our ways, and because of this he may not give us what we seek. Paul prayed and was heard, but his prayer could not command relief from his suffering, for there were wise purposes to be accomplished through his suffering. Christ in the garden prayed, and was heard in that he feared, but the cup was not taken away, for in his drinking that cup lay the fulfillment of God's mercy to men. The higher desire of the heart for holiness and for the best service may preclude the granting of the lower desire in the relief from suffering or the possession of some good.

THE PRAYERS OF THE BIBLE.

Many of the prayers of the Bible are wonderful in the boldness with which the petitioners approach God, and the confidence with which they expect an answer. As we read we are amazed and hesitate to follow, and yet they are inspired and approved examples for us. They show that the words of our Lord, "Ask what ye will," are to be taken in their fullest meaning. Not simply for the supply of our wants may we ask, but for the fulfillment of the highest desires of the soul and the gift of what we can neither comprehend nor define, but for which the renewed soul longs— the fullness of spiritual life. Not simply according to our asking, but far more exceedingly above all that we can ask or think does God give. Not by our need are we limited, but only by the riches of God's grace and his power to enlarge our capacities and to fill them with himself. Thus the apostle prays the God and Father of our Lord Jesus Christ that his Ephesian brethren may be filled " with all the fullness of God."

These prayers show us, also, with what boldness we may come to the throne of grace. David, penitent, prostrate and trembling, cries to God for mercy; but he rises, as he prays to the full confidence of one who knows his Father's love. Moses enters the cloud and talks with God "face to face, as a man with his friend." Paul prays as one who has been in the " third heavens." Nor is there in this aught of irreverence or presumption. With all humility in their boldness the petitioners stand before God in their sonship, and know they do not intrude upon a forbidden presence.

They do so with assurance that they will be heard.

They ask great things, but they know that they ask of a great God who has illimitable riches for his people. They come as accepted in the Beloved, and confidently plead his merits and his promises.

It is also to be observed, that at their highest point these prayers all meet in a common desire to know and enjoy God. For this David thirsted. It was the one supreme desire of Paul's heart. When Moses stood before the Lord in the mountain, perplexed as to duty, oppressed with a sense of human sinfulness and of divine justice, his prayer was: "Show me thy way and let me know thee; Show me thy glory." Here all prayers ultimately meet, for this is the tendency of the renewed nature; by this we are conformed to the divine image, and in this alone are we satisfied.

THE LORD'S PRAYER.

The most remarkable prayer is The Lord's Prayer. No prayer is so often repeated as this. It should not be repeated mechanically, without serious impressions as to the meaning of the words. Thus repeated it is only a lip service, and not a heartfelt prayer. Such a prayer cannot be acceptable to God, nor answered at the Throne of Grace.

"And it came to pass that as he was praying in a certain place, when he ceased, one of his disciples said unto him, Lord, teach us to pray, as John also taught his disciples. And he said unto them,

After this manner, therefore pray ye." Matt. vi. 9.

OUR FATHER, who art in heaven, hallowed be thy name; thy kingdom come; thy will be done on earth as it is in heaven. Give us this day our daily bread; and forgive us our trespasses, as we forgive those who have trespassed against us. And lead us not into temptation, but deliver us from evil: for thine is the kingdom, and the power, and the glory, forever. Amen.

The Lord's Prayer is divided into 1. The Introduction, 2. Seven Petitions, and 3. The Conclusion, or Doxology.

Introduction. Our Father, who art in heaven.

First Petition. Hallowed be Thy Name.

Second Petition. Thy Kingdom come,

Third Petition. Thy will be done on earth, as it is in heaven,

Fourth Petition. Give us this day our daily bread,

Fifth Petition. And forgive us our trespasses as we forgive those who have trespassed against us.

Sixth Petition. And lead us not into temptation.

Seventh Petition. But deliver us from evil.

Conclusion. For thine is the Kingdom, and the Power, and the Glory, forever and ever. Amen.

The Savior then adds these words, For if ye forgive men their trespasses, your heavenly Father will also forgive you; but if ye forgive not men their trespasses, neither will your Father forgive your trespasses. Matt. vi. 14, 15.

CHRIST'S PRAYER ON THE NIGHT IN WHICH HE WAS BETRAYED.

Father, the hour is come; glorify thy Son, that thy Son may also glorify thee: As thou hast given him power over all flesh, that he should give eternal life to as many as thou hast given him. And this is life eternal, that they might know thee, the only true God, and Jesus Christ whom thou hast sent.

I have glorified thee on the earth, I have finished the work which thou hast given me to do. And now, O Father, glorify thou me with thine own self, with the glory which I had with thee before the world was. I have manifested thy name unto the men, which thou gavest me out of the world; thine they were, and thou gavest them to me; and they have kept thy word. Now they have known that all things whatsoever thou hast given me are of thee. For I have given unto them the words which thou gavest me; and they have received them, and have known surely, that I have come out from thee, and they have believed that thou hast sent me. I pray for them; I pray not for the world, but for them which thou hast given me; for they are thine. And all mine are thine, and thine are mine; and I am glorified in them.

And now I am no more in the world, but these are in the world, and I come to thee. Holy Father, keep through thine own name those whom thou hast given me, that they may be one, as we are. While I was with them in the world, I kept them in thy name; those that thou gavest me I have kept, and none of them is lost but the son of perdition; that the Scripture might be fulfilled. And now come I to thee; and these things I speak in the world, that they might have my joy fulfilled in themselves, I have given them thy word; and the world hath hated them, because they are not of the world, even as I am not of the world. I pray not that thou shouldst take them out of the world, but that thou shouldest keep them from the evil. They are not of the world, even as I am not of the world. Sanctify them through thy truth; thy word is truth.

Neither pray I for them alone, but for them also, which shall believe on me through their word. That they all may be one; as thou, Father, art in me, and I in thee, that they also may be one in us; that the world may believe that thou hast sent me. And the glory which thou gavest me I have given them; that they may be one, even as we are one; I in thee, and thou in me, that they may be made perfect in one; and that the world may know, that thou hast sent me, and hast loved them, as thou hast loved me.

Father, I will that they also, whom thou hast given me, be with me where I am; that they may behold my glory, which thou hast given me; for thou lovedst me before the foundation of the world. Oh righteous Father, the world hath not known thee; but I have known thee, and these have known that thou hast sent me. And I have declared unto them thy name, and will declare it; that the love wherewith thou hast loved me, may be in them and I in thee.

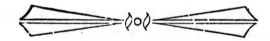

REMARKABLE PRAYERS.

LUTHER'S PRAYER AT THE DIET OF WORMS.

Before Luther went to the Diet he offered up the following prayer, which was overheard and recorded by his friends, and it is a touching and sublime prayer. We translate this prayer as literally as possible from the original German.

"Oh God! oh God! oh thou my God, do thou stand by me against the reason and wisdom of the whole world, do thou do it! Thou must stand by me, and thou alone! This is not my work, but thine. I have nothing to do here, before these great lords of the world on my own account. I would gladly pass my days in rest and peace, and be unmolested. But the cause is thine, O Lord! and it is a righteous and everlasting cause. But do thou support me, O thou faithful and eternal God. I depend on no human aid. Hast not thou called me to this work, and I am certain of it! Yes, this is thy will. This is not my doing, I never thought of myself to oppose such great lords. So do thou support me for the sake of thy dear Son Jesus Christ, who shall be my protector, my defence, and my strong tower, through the power, and strength of the Holy Ghost! Lord where remainest thou? Thou my God, where art thou? Come, oh come, I am ready to lay down my life with the patience of a lamb, for this is a righteous cause, and it is thy cause. I will never be separated from thee. This I have resolved upon in thy name; the world shall never force my conscience, and if it were full of devils

—and if this body which is the work of thine hands, should be trodden down upon the earth, and be cut to pieces ;. for I have thine own word and Spirit for this. Not only the body, but the soul is thine, and will be thine forever. Amen. God help me. Amen."

A PRAYER OF S. S. SCHMUCKER WHILE UNDER CONVICTION.

While Principal of the York County Academy in 1816, and in the 17th year of his age, he wrote the following penetential prayer in his diary:

Nov. 6. O Lord God, I am a sinner, and the iniquity of my ways will bring me to eternal ruin, if thy saving hand be not exerted in my favor. Though I am guilty of no crime against the world, or to my knowledge any individual, my heart is yet prone to evil and my ways are far from God. There was a time, O Lord, when I was much nearer to thee, than at present I am. Thou hast promised that "Whatsoever we ask of thee in the name of thy Son Jesus Christ shall be granted, that the Father may be glorified." Now Lord, I beseech thee, to change my heart, and give me a new and purified spirit! O Lord, numbers are rushing with me the road to perdition. Stretch forth thine all powerful hand, and arrest us in our mad carreer. We are seated in the chariot of iniquity, and are driving headlong to the gulf of destruction. Many times hast thou called us, but we heeded not thine admonitions ; nothing but thy divine interposition, O Lord, will save us !

Nov. 19. O Lord, blessed be thy holy name, that thou hast preserved us to this day; that thou has prolonged the duration of our existence until the present moment. How many have during the last night been transposed from time

to eternity! For how many was the race run and the thread
of life cut off? We, Lord, are yet spared; and to thine
unmerited kindness and forbearance are we indebted for it!
We have erred and gone astray; we have sinned against
thee; "there is not one that doeth good, no not one."
We are going the way of the iniquitous, and the path of the
Lord we know not. Soon will the earthly race be run, and
we go to another world, to receive the reward of our labor.
O God, our works have been of the flesh, and from the
flesh we would inherit eternal damnation. But thou hast
promised, that thou wilt hear the penitent, and the death of
the sinner thou wilt not. In thy promise alone do we repose the hope of our salvation,—in the promise of HIM,
who died for man, that he might never die! O that we
might see the folly of our ways and fly to thee for assistance!
But our nature is corrupted and we are prone to sin. But
do thou, Lord, pardon our manifold transgressions; and as
men will not obey thy commands, but are full of sin, do
thou rule us with a rod of iron, and put a bit into our
mouths, which will certainly bring us to reason. Yet, O
Lord, thy punishments are severe, I feel the hand of the
Lord upon me; I am sorely afflicted and ready to bend
down under the load of affliction. "My soul is exceedingly
sorrowful, even unto death." "O Lord, wilt thou not
deliver me?"

Nov. 20. On the morning of this day, O merciful Creator, how should I glorify thy name, that thou hast spared me
until this day. My life has been an uninterrupted scene of
ungodliness, and my heart knows not God. With guilt upon
my head, contrition of my heart, Oh how could I have met
and stood before my Judge, had I died during the last
night. Thou, O Lord, hast spared my life, and on the
morning of this day hast condescended to assuage in some

degree, the misery of my condition, and given another day for the salvation of my soul. O Lord, blessed be thy name, for the unmerited blessings which thou hast been pleased to bestow upon me. Grant that it may not arise in evidence against me on the great and awful day of Judgment. That I may apply it to the working out of the salvation of my soul, and the abstraction of my mind from the idleness of this world. Lord, I desire to be saved; my soul longs to be wrested from the flames in which it is now consuming. But I am weak and miserable, for the grace of God is not upon me. Within these five years, to the best of my recollection, thou Lord knowest, I have made about 100 attempts and commencements at conversion, but the work was always prevented by my own evil doings. I did not permit God to direct me, but was always determined to go according to my own head. Lord, now I am convinced of my own inability, and come entirely to thee. Do thou direct me; be thou my leader, and form my heart, such as thou wilt have it should be. Thy blessed word teaches us, that salvation of souls is not the work of man; nay, if all the angels in heaven united their strength, it would not be sufficient for the salvation of one soul! Man is mortal; angels approach the divine nature to an amazing degree, and are therefore far greater than man; but angels are incompetent to the salvation of a soul; how can man, who is so far inferior to angels, do anything towards the accomplishment of this divine purpose! O Lord, therefore I will submit solely to thy direction, and trust in thy promise, that thou wilt convert me, and conduct all things in such a manner, as finally to end in my salvation. Amen.

A BEAUTIFUL MARRIAGE PRAYER.

Would that every marriage might be marked with the lofty purpose and serious earnestness that characterized the union of William Cullen Bryant and Fanny Fairchild. After Mr. Bryant's death this recorded prayer, relating to his marriage was found in his private papers:

"May God Almighty mercifully take care of our happiness here and hereafter. May we ever continue constant to each other, and mindful of our mutual promises of attachment and truth. In due time, if it be the will of Providence, may we become more nearly connected with each other, and together may we lead a long, happy and innocent life, without any diminution of affection until we die. May there never be any jealousy, distrust, coldness, or dissatisfaction between us, nor occasion for any—nothing but kindness, forbearance, mutual confidence, and attention to each other's happiness. And that we may be less unworthy of so great a blessing, may we be assisted to cultivate all the benign and charitable affections and offices, not only toward each other, but toward our neighbors, the human race, and all the creatures of God. And in all things wherein we have done ill, may we properly repent of our error, and may God forgive us, and dispose us to do better. When at last we are called to render back the life we have received, may our deaths be peaceful and may God take us to his bosom. All which may he grant for the sake of the Messiah."

Husband and wife walked together for forty five years, and their way became more and more beautiful as the days and months and years went by.

PRAYER AT THE THIRD CENTURIAL JUBILEE OF THE REFORMATION, OCT. 31ST, 1817.

BY REV. F. C. SCHAEFFER, D. D.

Thee, the Eternal and Exalted—thee, the only true God we adore !—Unto thee, the almighty, all-wise and all-gracious God and Father, we give thanks, that thou hadst tender pity upon thy church ; that through chosen instruments thou didst restore, and hast hitherto preserved the truths of thy gospel. We beseech thee, guide us by thy Spirit, that the present solemn occasion may be sanctified unto us—that we may continually confide in thy truth, willingly follow after the light of thy gospel—prove the fruits of our faith with an holy conversation, and, finally, depart hence in peace, through Jesus Christ, thy Son, our Lord and Savior.

Yea, great things hast thou done, O gracious God and Father, for thy people ! Thou hast made thy wonderful works to be remembered; they shall never be forgotten. By thy omnipotence thou didst deliver our ancestors from the power of darkness ; thou didst bless them with the knowledge of truth, and didst translate them into the kingdom of thy dear Son; *in whom* we have redemption through his blood, even the forgiveness of sins. Unto this day hast thou preserved these benefits to thy church, and therewith hast thou also favored us, whereof we are glad and rejoice before thee. Oh Lord, preserve unto us thy word, for it is unto us the joy and rejoicing of our hearts. Preserve this rich treasure unto us, and to all who may succeed us. When centuries after centuries have descended into the depths of time, may thy people ever be enabled to rejoice, and to declare in truth on days similar to the one which now exhilarates our hearts : Thy word, O

Lord, thy saving gospel is pure and undefiled amongst us until this day. We beseech thee, Father, let the light of thy gospel illuminate the world more and more, and shed its rays over all the nations of the earth. Do thou assist thy messengers and servants, who proclaim thy name, and preach thy holy religion, that they, and those who hear them, may glorify thee, and be saved through faith in Jesus Christ, and him crucified. Grant us thy grace, that we may faithfully cleave unto thy gospel, walk worthy of the same, and at last die in its comforts, cheerful and happy, through Jesus Christ thy Son, our Lord,—then will we in a better world join with all the company of heaven, in the song of praise and of thy divine glory.

Holy, holy, holy, Lord God of hosts, heaven and earth are full of thy glory. Glory be to thee, O Lord most high.

O holy God, the Creator!
O holy God, the Mediator!
O holy God, the Merciful Comforter!
Thou Eternal and Exalted God!
Evermore grant us thy peace.   Amen.

PRAYER AT A TEMPERANCE MEETING.

O Lord, God, thou holy, just and righteous Jehovah, we come before thee to implore thy blessing upon the object of our assembly. Thou abhorest iniquity and crime in all their forms, and thou art merciful and compassionate to all the suffering and oppressed sons and daughters of mankind. We pray thee, look in pity on the families, the wives, and children, and relatives of the thousands of drunkards in our land; send them relief in their distress and help from on high.

Have mercy on the poor drunkard; enable him to see and realize his great guilt and danger, and that unless he shall repent and reform he must inevitably perish, both in body and in soul; for thy word assures us, that no drunkard shall enter into the kingdom of God. May he therefore repent of his sin, and in reliance on thy divine help, " Look not upon the intoxicating wine," much less taste or drink it, for in the end it biteth like a serpent and stingeth like an adder.

O Lord, we deplore the prevalence of intemperance in every part of the world, and especially do we lament its dessolating effect in our own beloved country. While we boast of our civil and religious liberty, yet, O how many thousands are slaves to a dreadful appetite, which involves them in sin and shame, and their families in poverty and misery.

We deplore the fact that our own government is the chief partner in this iniquitous traffic, by legalizing the manufacture and sale of intoxicants, and licensing the evil for the sake of money, and thus drawing its revenues from the crimes, poverty and misery of its own citizens.

We pray that the eyes of the people of this nation may be opened, and their consciences awakened, and that they

may be induced to abstain entirely from the use of intoxicants as a beverage.   Especially may the young and rising
generation, the hope of the church and the country, grow
up in the love and practice of temperance, and total abstinence from strong drink.

We pray that the conscience of the dealers in strong
drink may be awakened to see their awful guilt before God,
their Maker and their final Judge, who has declared a woe
upon him that putteth his bottle to his neighbor and maketh
him drunk.   May they see themselves in the light that God
sees them, and abandon that business which brings so
much crime, poverty and misery upon mankind.

We pray for our rulers and legislators, who make
the laws under which this evil traffic is licensed and carried
on.   May they realize that they have been elected to make
laws for the good of the people, and not for their corruption
and demoralization.   May they be mindful of the truth that
there is a higher Lawgiver above them, who will hold them
responsible for their actions at his judgement bar.

And we pray, that the people who by their votes elect
the legislators, may be careful and conscientious, not to elect
such men to make our laws, as are influenced by selfish
motives and personal gain, but such as are patriotic and
God fearing men, who have the fear of God in their hearts,
and who will enact such laws as will promote morality and
prosperity, and shield the people from temptation and ruin.

May we also have such officers appointed, who will
faithfully enforce the laws that are enacted for the good of
society, and who will not connive at existing evils, or take
bribes to shield the guilty.

We pray that the governments of the world, and
especially our own government may see the enormous evil
of sending great shiploads of strong drink to heathen lands;
which tends so greatly to debauch still more the poor

benighted heathen, and thus hinder the progress of Christianity and civilization in those dark places of the earth, where the church is sending Bibles and missionaries to bring them the light of the gospel.

O Lord God, how long shall this dreadful traffic continue? O do thou exert thine almighty power to stay the prevalence of wickedness of every kind. Let Satan's kingdom be destroyed, the kingdom of grace advanced, and the kingdom of glory hastened; in the name of Jesus Christ. Amen.

A REMARKABLE OLD PRAYER.

Here is a prayer, " set forth by order of King Edward the Sixth," of England, about the year 1550, more than two hundred and fifty years ago. Yet it suits our times very well now by a little change in the wording. For example, substitute for " them that possess the pasters and grounds of the earth," the words " all employers of labor," and this prayer will fit the times we live in, in America :

" We heartily pray thee to send thy Holy Spirit into the hearts of them that possess the pasters and grounds of the earth, that they, remembering themselves to be thy tenants, may not rack or stretch out the rents of their houses or lands, nor yet take unreasonable fines or moneys, after the manner of covetous worldlings; but so let them out that the inhabitants thereof may be able to pay the rents, and to live and nourish their families, grace, also, to consider that they are but strangers and pilgrims in this world, having here no dwelling place, but seeking one to come; that they, remembering the short continuance of this life, may be content with that which is sufficient, and not join house to house and land to land to the impoverishment of others; but so behave themselves in letting their tenements, lands and pasters that, after this life, they may be received into everlasting habitations."

GRACE AT TABLE.

The eyes of all wait upon thee, O Lord; Thou givest them their meat in due season. Thou openest thine hand and satisfiest the desires of every living thing.

O Lord God, our Heavenly Father, bless this food to our nourishment, and may it strengthen us in the doing of thy holy will, through Christ our Savior. Amen.

Our Father who art in heaven, bless the provisions of thy bounty now set before us, and feed our souls with the bread of life, for Christ's sake. Amen.

GRACE AFTER MEALS.

We thank thee, Heavenly Father, that thou hast again supplied our bodily wants. Continue to supply all our wants, both of body and soul. We ask it for Christ's sake. Amen.

Blessed be the Lord, who daily loadeth us with benefits. Ps. lx. 19.

O give thanks unto the Lord, for his mercy endureth forever. Amen.

CHILD'S MORNING PRAYERS.

Now I am wakened out of sleep,
I pray *thee*, Lord, my soul to keep,
If I should die before the eve,
I pray *thee*, Lord, my soul receive,
That I may with my Savior live. Amen.

Now I wake and see the light,
'Tis God has kept me through the night,
To him I lift my hands and pray,
That he would keep me through this day,
And if I die before 'tis done,
Great God, accept me, through thy Son. Amen.

Every day will I bless thee; I will praise thy name forever and ever. Ps. cxlv. 2.

I laid me down and slept; I awaked, for the Lord sustained me. Ps. ii. 5. Amen.

Unto thee do I lift up mine eyes, O thou that dwellest, in the heavens. Ps. cxxiii. 1. Amen.

CHILD'S EVENING PRAYERS.

Now I lay me down to sleep,
I pray *thee*, Lord, my soul to keep;
If I should die before I wake,
I pray *thee*, Lord, my soul to take,
And this I ask for Jesus' sake. Amen·

Forgive, O Lord, for thy dear Son,
The ill that I this day have done;
That with the world, myself and thee,
I, ere I sleep, at peace may be. Amen.

Jesus, tender Shepherd, hear me,
Bless thy little child to-night,
Through the darkness be thou near me,
Keep me safe till morning light.

All this day thy hand has led me,
And I thank thee for thy care;
Thou hast warmed me, clothed me, fed me,
Listen to my evening prayer.

May my sins be all forgiven,
Bless the friends I love so well,
Take me, Lord, at last to heaven,
Happy there with thee to dwell. Amen.

HYMNS.

MORNING HYMNS.

Another six days' work is done,   L. M.
Another Sabbath is begun :
Return, my soul, enjoy thy rest,
Improve the day thy God has blest.

Come, bless the Lord, whose love assigns
So sweet a rest to wearied minds ;
Provides an antepast of heav'n,
And gives this day the food of sev'n.

O that our thoughts and thanks may rise
As grateful incense to the skies ;
And draw from heaven that sweet repose
Which none, but he who feels it, knows.

What a friend we have in Jesus,
  All our sins and griefs to bear ;
What a privilege to carry
  Everything to God in prayer.
Oh, what peace we often forfeit,
  Oh, what needless pain we bear—
All because we do not carry
  Everything to God in prayer.

Have we trials and temptations?
  Is there trouble anywhere?
We should never be discouraged,
  Take it to the Lord in prayer.
Can we find a Friend so faithful,
  Who will all our sorrows share?
Jesus knows our every weakness,
  Take it to the Lord in prayer.

Awake, my soul, and with the sun   L. M.
Thy daily stage of duty run ;
Shake off dull sloth, and joyful rise
To pay thy morning sacrifice.

By influence of the light divine,
Let thy own light to others shine ;
Reflect all heaven's propitious rays
In ardent love and cheerful praise.

Lord ! I my vows to thee renew :
Disperse my sins as morning dew ;
Guard my first springs of thought and will,
And with thyself my spirit fill.

Rock of ages ! cleft for me,   7s.
Let me hide myself in thee !
Let the Water and the Blood,
From thy riven side that flowed,
Be of sin the double cure ;
Save me, Lord, and make me pure.

Nothing in my hand I bring,
Simply to thy cross I cling ;
Naked, come to thee for dress';
Helpless, look to thee for grace ;
Foul, I to the Fountain fly ;
Wash me, Savior, or I die !

There is a fountain filled with blood   C. M.
 Drawn from Immanuel's veins ;
And sinners plunged beneath that flood
 Lose all their guilty stains.

The dying thief rejoiced to see
 That fountain in his day ;
Oh, there may I, though vile as he,
 Wash all my sins away !

Dear dying Lamb, thy precious blood
 Shall never lose its power,
Till all the ransom'd church of God
 Be saved, to sin no more.

Savior, like a Shepherd lead us,   8s, 7s & 4.
 Much we need thy tend'rest care ;
In thy pleasant pastures feed us,
 For our use thy folds prepare ;
  Blessed Jesus,
 Thou hast bought us, thine we are.

Thou hast promised to receive us,
 Poor and sinful though we be ;
Thou hast mercy to relieve us,
 Grace to cleanse, and power to free ;
  Blessed Jesus,
 Let us early turn to thee.

I heard the voice of Jesus say,   C. M. D.
. "Come unto me and rest;
Lay down, thou weary one, lay down
  Thy head upon my breast?"
I came to Jesus as I was,
  Weary, and worn, and sad;
I found in him a resting-place,
  And he has made me glad.

I heard the voice of Jesus say,
. "Behold, I freely give
The living water; thirsty one,
  Stoop down, and drink, and live!"
I came to Jesus, and I drank
  Of that life-giving stream;
My thirst was quench'd, my soul revived,
  And now I live in him.

EVENING HYMNS.

Softly fades the twilight ray   7s.
Of the holy Sabbath day;
Gently as life's setting sun,
When the Christian's course is run.

Peace is on the world abroad;
'Tis the holy peace of God—
Symbol of the peace within,
When the spirit rests from sin.

Savior, may our Sabbaths be
Days of peace and joy in thee;
Till in heaven our souls repose,
Where the Sabbath ne'er shall close.

The day is past and gone,   S. M.
  The evening shades appear,
Oh, may I ever keep in mind
  The night of death draws near.

Lord, keep me safe this night,
  Secure from all my fears;
May angels guard me while I sleep,
  Till morning light appears.

And when I early rise,
  To view th' unwearied sun,
May I set out to win the prize,
  And after glory run.

Thus far the Lord has led me on;   L. M.
  Thus far his power prolongs my days
And every ev'ning shall make known
  Some fresh memorial of his grace.

Much of my time has run to waste,
  And I, perhaps, am near my home;
But he forgives my follies past,
  And strength supplies for days to come.

I lay my body down to sleep;
  Peace is the pillow of my head:
His ever-watchful eye will keep
  Its constant guard around my bed.

Faith in his name forbids my fear;
  Oh, may thy presence ne'er depart!
And in the morning may I bear
  Thy loving-kindness on my heart.

Nearer, my God, to thee,   6s & 4s.
  Nearer to thee!
E'en though it be a cross
  That raiseth me;
Still all my song shall be,
  Nearer, my God, to thee,
Nearer to thee!

Though like a wanderer,
The sun gone down,
  Darkness be over me,
My rest a stone;
  Yet in my dreams I'd be,
Nearer, my God, to thee,
  Nearer to thee!

Glory to thee, my God, this night,   L. M.
For all the blessings of the light;
Keep me, oh, keep me, King of kings,
Under thine own almighty wings.

Teach me to live, that I may dread
The grave as little as my bed ;
Teach me to die, that so I may
With joy behold the judgment-day.

Praise God, from whom all blessings flow ;
Praise him, all creatures here below ;
Praise him above, ye heavenly host,
Praise Father, Son and Holy Ghost.

Jesus lover of my soul,   7s.
    Let me to thy bosom fly,
While the nearer waters roll,
    While the tempest still is high :
Hide me, O my Savior, hide,
    Till the storm of life is past;
Safe into the haven guide ;
    Oh, receive my soul at last !

Other refuge have I none ;
    Hangs my helpless soul on thee :
Leave, Oh, leave me not alone,
    Still support and comfort me :
All my trust on thee is stay'd,
    All my help from thee I bring ;
Cover my defenseless head
    With the shadow of thy wing.

Jesus ! I live to thee,   6s & 7s.
    The loveliest and best ;
My life in thee, thy life in me,
    In thy blest love I rest.

Jesus ! I die to thee
    Whenever death shall come ;
To die in thee is life to me
    In my eternal home.

Whether to live or die,
    I know not which is best ;
To live in thee is bliss to me,
    To die is endless rest.

Living or dying, Lord !
    I ask but to be thine ;
My life in thee, thy life in me,
    Makes heaven for ever mine.
                      Rev. H. Harbaugh.

TABLE OF CONTENTS.

	PAGE.
Preface	iii
The Lord's Prayer	5
Scriptural Forms of Blessing	5

MORNING AND EVENING PRAYERS.

First Week	6
Second Week	34
Third Week	62
Fourth Week	90
Fifth Week	118

PRAYERS FOR SPECIAL OCCASIONS.

Christmas Day	146
The Last Day of the Year	148
The First Morning of the New Year	150
Good Friday	152
Easter Day	154
Ascension Day	156
Whitsunday, or Pentecost	158
Prayer for a Day of Humiliation	161
Prayer for a Day of Thanksgiving	162
Anniversary of the Reformation	164
Morning of a Communion Sabbath	166
Evening of a Communion Sabbath	168
For a Time of Bereavement	170
Prayer to be Used by a Family Detained From Public Worship	172
Prayer to be Used at the Bedside of a Dying Believer	174
Prayer to be Uttered by the Sick	176
Prayer of Parents for their Children	177
A prayer to be Used by the Children	181
Another Prayer for Children	183
Prayers for Opening a Sunday-school	186
Prayers for Closing a Sunday-school	194
Matthias Claudius Exposition of the Lord's Prayer	202
A Paraphrase of the Lord's Prayer	205
Another Paraphrase of the Lord's Prayer	206
A Dissertation on Prayer, BY MATTHEW HENRY	208

	PAGE.
The Limitations of Prayer	215
THE PRAYERS OF THE BIBLE	217
The Lord's Prayer	218
Christ's Prayer on the Night in which He was Betrayed	219

REMARKABLE PRAYERS.

Luther's Prayer at the Diet of Worms	222
Prayers of S S. Schmucker, When Under Conviction	223
A Beautiful Marriage Prayer	226
Prayer at the Third Centurial Jubilee of the Reformation, Oct. 31st, 1817	227
Prayer at a Temperance Meeting	229
A Remarkable Old Prayer	231
Grace at Table	232
Grace After Meals	232
Child's Morning Prayers	232
Child's Evening Prayers	233
Morning Hymns	234
Evening Hymns	236

TABLE OF SCRIPTURE READING LESSONS.

A portion of the Holy Scripture should be read in connection with every act of Family Worship. The following table, taken from the "*Home Altar*," by Dr. Deems, will give the lessons which embrace those portions of sacred Scripture, likely to be most profitable, when read at Family Worship. The lessons extend over two years. "No table could be constructed for one year, without making the lessons unsuitably and unprofitably long."

FIRST YEAR.

CALENDAR.	MORNING.	EVENING.
JANUARY 1	GENESIS 1	MATTHEW 1
" 2	" 2	" 2
" 3	" 3	" 3
" 4	" 4	" 4
.. 5	" 5	" 5 to v. 21
" 6	" 6	" 5 v. 21
" 7	" 7	" 6 to v. 16
" 8	" 8	" 6 v. 16
9	" 9	" 7
" 10	" 10	" 8 to v. 18
" 11	" 12	" 8 v. 18
" 12	" 13	" 9 to v. 18
" 13	" 14	" 9 v. 18
" 14	" 15	" 10
" 15	" 16	" 11
" 16	" 17	" 12 to v. 22
" 17	" 18 to v. 17	" 12 v. 22
" 18	" 18 v. 17	" 13 to v. 31
" 19	" 19 to v. 30	" 13 v. 31
" 20	" 20	" 14
" 21	" 21 to v. 22	" 15 to v. 21
" 22	" 21 v. 22	" 15 v. 21
" 23	" 22	" 16
" 24	" 23	" 17
" 25	" 24 to v. 32	" 18 to v. 21
" 26	" 24 v. 32	" 18 v. 21
" 27	" 25 to v. 19	" 19
" 28	" 25 v. 19	" 20 to v. 17
" 29	" 26 to v. 17	" 20 v. 17
" 30	" 26 v. 17	" 21 to v. 23
" 31	" 27 to v. 30	" 21 v. 23
FEBRUARY 1	" 27 v. 30	" 22 to v. 23
" 2	" 28	" 22 v. 23
" 3	" 29 to v. 15	" 23
" 4	" 29 v. 15	" 24
" 5	" 30 to v. 25	" 25 to v. 31

FIRST YEAR.

CALENDAR.	MORNING.	EVENING.
FEBRUARY 6	GENESIS 30 v. 25	MATTHEW 25 v. 31
" 7	" 31 to v. 25	" 26 to v. 36
" 8	" 32 to v. 24	" 26 v. 36
" 9	" 32 v. 24	" 27
" 10	" 33	" 28
" 11	" 34	MARK 1
" 12	" 35	" 2
" 13	" 37	" 3
" 14	" 39	' 4 to v. 26
" 15	" 40	" 4 v. 26
" 16	" 41 to v. 37	" 5 to v. 21
" 17	" 41 v. 37	" 5 v 21
" 18	" 42 to v. 25	" 6 to v 30
" 19	" 42 v. 25	" 6 v. 30
" 20	" 43 to v. 15	" 7 to v. 24
" 21	" 43 v. 15	" 7 v. 24
" 22	" 44 to v. 14	" 8 to v. 27
" 23	" 44 v. 14	" 8 v. 27
" 24	" 45 to v. 16	" 9 to v. 30
" 25	" 45 v. 16	" 9 v. 30
" 26	" 46	" 10 to v. 32
" 27	" 47	" 10 v. 32
" 28	" 48	" 11
MARCH 1	" 49	" 12
" 2	" 50 to v. 15	" 13
" 3	" 50 v. 15	" 14 to v. 26
4	EXODUS 1	" 14 v. 26
5	" 2	" 15
6	" 3	" 16
" 7	" 4 to v. 18	LUKE 1 to v. 39
" 8	" 4 v. 18	" 1 v. 39
9	" 5	" 2 to v. 40
10	" 6 to v. 14	" 2 v. 40
" 11	" 6 v. 14	" 3
" 12	" 7	" 4
" 13	" 8 to v. 16	" 5
" 14	" 8 v. 16	" 6 to v. 20
" 15	" 9 to v. 13	" 6 v. 20
" 16	" 9 v. 13	" 7 to v. 36
" 17	" 10 to v. 12	" 7 v. 36
" 18	" 10 v. 12	" 8 to v. 26
" 19	" 11	" 8 v. 26
" 20	" 12 to v. 37	" 9 to v. 37
" 21	" 12 v. 37	" 9 v. 37
" 22	" 13	" 10 to v 25
" 23	" 14 to v. 15	" 10 v. 25
" 24	" 14 v. 15	" 11 to v. 29

FIRST YEAR.

CALENDAR.		MORNING.		EVENING.	
MARCH	25	EXODUS	15	LUKE	11 v. 29
"	26	"	16	"	12
"	27	"	17	"	13
"	28	"	18	"	14
"	29	"	19	"	15
"	30	"	20	"	16
"	31	"	21 to v. 18	"	17 to v. 20
APRIL	1	"	21 v. 18	"	17 v. 20
"	2	"	22 to v. 16	"	18 to v. 31
"	3	"	22 v. 16	"	18 v. 31
"	4	"	23 to v. 20	"	19 to v. 28
"	5	"	23 v. 20	"	19 v. 28
"	6	"	24	"	20
"	7	"	32 to v. 15	"	21
"	8	"	32 v. 15	"	22 to v. 31
"	9	"	33	"	22 v. 31
"	10	"	34 to v. 27	"	23
"	11	"	34 v. 27	"	24
"	12	"	40	JOHN	1 to v. 29
"	13	LEVITI.	19 to v. 19	"	1 v. 29
"	14	"	19 v. 19	"	2
"	15	"	24		3 to v. 22
"	16	"	25		3 v. 22
"	17	"	26 to v. 21	"	4
"	18	"	26 v. 21	"	5
"	19	NUMBERS	11 to v. 24	"	6 to v. 22
"	20	"	11 v. 24	"	6 v. 22
"	21	"	12	"	7 to v. 32
"	22	"	13	"	7 v. 32
"	23	"	14 to v. 26	"	8 to v. 21
"	24	"	14 v. 26	"	8 v. 21
"	25	"	16 to v. 36	"	9
"	26	"	16 v. 36	"	10 to v. 22
"	27	"	17	"	10 v. 22
"	28	"	20	"	11 to v. 30
"	29	"	21	"	11 v. 30
"	30	"	22	"	12 to v. 20
MAY	1	"	23	"	12 v. 20
"	2	"	24	"	13
"	3	"	25	"	14
"	4	"	27	"	15
"	5	"	30	"	16
"	6	"	31 to v. 25	"	17
"	7	"	31 v. 25	"	18
"	8	"	32	"	19
"	9	"	35	"	20
"	10	"	36	"	21

FIRST YEAR

CALENDAR.		MORNING.		EVENING.	
MAY	11	DEUT.	1 to v. 19	ACTS	1
"	12	"	1 v. 19	"	2
"	13	"	2 to v. 26	"	3
	14	"	2 v. 26	"	4 to v. 23
	15	"	3		4 v. 23
"	16	"	4 to v. 25	"	5 to v. 17
	17	"	4 v. 25		5 v. 17
	18	"	5 to v. 22	"	6
"	19	"	5 v. 22	"	7 to v. 30
	20	"	6		7 v. 30
"	21	"	7		8 to v. 26
"	22	"	8	"	8 v. 26
"	23	"	9		9 to v. 23
"	24	"	10	"	9 v. 23
"	25	"	11	"	10 to v. 34
"	26	"	12	"	10 v. 34
	27	"	13	"	11 to v. 19
"	28	"	14	"	11 v. 19
"	29	"	15	"	12
"	30	"	16	"	13 to v. 14
"	31	"	17	"	13 v. 14
JUNE	1	"	18	"	14 to v. 19
"	2	"	19	"	14 v. 19
"	3	"	20	"	15
"	4	"	21	"	16 to v. 14
"	5	"	22	"	16 v. 14
"	6	"	24	"	17 to v. 16
"	7	"	25	"	17 v. 16
"	8	"	26	"	18 to v. 18
	9	"	27	"	18 v. 18
	10	"	28 to v. 15	"	19 to v. 21
"	11	"	28 v. 15	"	19 v. 21
	12	"	29	"	20 to v. 17
	13	"	30	"	21
"	14	"	31	"	22
"	15	"	32	"	23
"	16	"	33	"	24
"	17	"	34	"	25
	18	JOSHUA	1	"	26
"	19	"	2	"	27 to v. 31
"	20	"	3	"	27 v. 31
	21	"	4	"	28 to v. 17
"	22	"	5	"	28 v. 17
	23	"	6 to v. 12	ROMANS	1
	24	"	6 v. 12	"	2
	25	"	7 to v. 16	"	3
	26	"	7 v. 16	"	4

FIRST YEAR.

CALENDAR.		MORNING.		EVENING.	
JUNE	27	JOSHUA	8 to v. 14	ROMANS	5
"	28	"	8 v. 14	"	6
"	29	"	9	"	7
"	30	"	10 to v. 15	"	8
JULY	1	"	10 v. 15 to 28	"	9
"	2	"	10 v. 28	"	10
"	3	"	22 to v. 21	"	11
"	4	"	22 v. 21	"	12
	5	"	23	"	13
	6	"	24 to v. 19	"	14
	7	"	24 v. 19	"	15
	8	JUDGES	1 to v. 22	"	16
	9	"	1 v. 22	1 COR.	1
"	10	"	2 to v. 11	"	2
"	11	"	2 v. 11	"	3
"	12	"	3 to v. 12	"	4
"	13	"	3 v. 12	"	5
"	14	"	4	"	6
"	15	"	5	"	7
"	16	"	6 to v. 11	"	8
"	17	"	6 v. 11 to 25	"	9
"	18	"	6 v. 25	"	10
"	19	"	7	"	11
"	20	"	8 to v. 22	"	12
"	21	"	8 v. 22	"	13
"	22	"	9 to v. 22	"	14
"	23	"	9 v. 22 to 46	"	15
"	24	"	9 v. 46	"	16
"	25	"	10	2 COR.	1
"	26	"	11 to v. 29	"	2
"	27	"	11 v. 29	"	3
"	28	"	12	"	4
"	29	"	13	"	5
"	30	"	14	"	6
"	31	"	15	"	7
AUGUST	1	"	16 to v. 21	"	8
"	2	"	16 v. 21	"	9
"	3	"	17	"	10
	4	"	18	"	11
	5	"	19 to v. 22	"	12
	6	"	19 v. 22	"	13
	7	"	20 to v. 26	GALAT'NS	1
	8	"	20 v. 26	"	2
	9	"	21 to v 16	"	3
"	10	"	21 v. 16		4
"	11	RUTH	1		5
"	12	"	2	"	6

FIRST YEAR.

CALENDAR.		MORNING.		EVENING.	
AUGUST	13	RUTH	3	EPHES.	1
"	14	"	4	"	2
"	15	1 SAMUEL	1	"	3
"	16	"	2 to v. 22	"	4
"	17	"	2 v. 22	"	5
"	18	"	3	"	6
"	19	"	4	PHIL.	1
	20	"	5	"	2
"	21	"	6	"	3
"	22	"	7	"	4
	23	"	8	COLOSS'NS	1
"	24	"	9	"	2
"	25	"	10	"	3
"	26	"	11	"	4
"	27	"	12	1 THES.	1
"	28	"	13	"	2
"	29	"	14 to v. 24	"	3
"	30	"	14 v. 24	"	4
"	31	"	15	"	5
SEPTEMB'R	1	"	16	2 THES.	1
"	2	"	17 to v. 30	"	2
"	3	"	17 v. 30	"	3
	4	"	18	1 TIM.	1
	5	"	19	"	2, 3
	6	"	20	"	4
"	7	"	21	"	5
"	8	"	22	"	6
"	9	"	23	2 TIM.	1
"	10	"	24	"	2
"	11	"	25	"	3
	12	"	26	"	4
	13	"	27	TITUS	1
	14	"	28	"	2, 3
"	15	"	29	PHILEMON	
	16	"	30	HEBREWS	1
"	17	"	31	"	2
"	18	2 SAMUEL	1	"	3
	19	"	2		4
"	20	"			5
"	21	"			6
	22	"	4		7
	23	"	5		8
	24	"	7		9
"	25	"	8	"	10
	26	"		"	11
"	27	"	10	"	12
	28	"	11	"	13

FIRST YEAR.

CALENDAR.		MORNING.		EVENING.	
SEPT.	29	2 SAMUEL 12		JAMES	1
"	30	"	13 to v. 23	"	2
OCTOBER	1	"	13 v. 23	"	3
"	2	"	14	"	4
"	3	"	15	"	5
	4	"	16	1 PETER	1
	5	"	17	"	2
	6	"	18	"	3
	7	"	19 to v. 16	"	4
	8	'	19 v. 16	"	5
	9	"	20	2 PETER	1
"	10	"	21	"	2
"	11	"	22	"	3
	12	"	23	1 JOHN	1
"	13	"	24	"	2
"	14	1 KINGS 1 to v. 28		"	3
"	15	"	1 v. 28	"	4
"	16	'	2 to v. 26	"	5
"	17	"	2 v. 26	2, 3 JOHN	
"	18	"	3	JUDE	
"	19	"	4	REV.	1
"	20	"	5	"	2
"	21	"	6	"	3
"	22	"	7	"	4, 5
"	23	"	8	"	6
"	24	"	9	"	7
"	25	"	10	"	8
"	26	"	11 to v. 26	"	9
"	27	"	11 v. 26	"	10
	28	"	12	"	11
"	29	"	13	"	12
"	30	"	14	"	13
"	31	"	15	"	14
NOVEMB'R	1	"	16	"	15
"	2	"	17	"	16
"	3	"	18	"	17
	4	"	19	"	18
	5	"	20 to v. 22	"	19
"	6	"	20 v. 22	"	20
	7	"	21	"	21
	8	"	22 to v. 29	"	22
	9	"	22 v. 29	PSALM	1
"	10	2 KINGS 1		"	2
"	11	"	2	"	3
"	12	"	3	"	4
"	13	"	4	"	6
"	14	"	5		7

FIRST YEAR.

CALENDAR.	MORNING.		EVENING.	
NOVEMB'R 15	2 KINGS	6	PSALM	8
" 16	"	7	"	9
" 17	"	8	"	10
18	"	9	"	11
19	"	10	"	12
" 20	"	11	"	13
" 21	"	12	"	14
22	"	13	"	15
23	"	14	"	16
" 24	"	15	"	17
" 25	"	16	"	18 to v. 24
" 26	"	17 to v. 24	"	18 v. 24
27	"	17 v. 24	"	19
28	"	18	"	20
29	"	19 to v. 20	"	21
" 30	"	19 v. 20	"	22 to v. 18
DECEMBER 1	"	20	"	22 v. 18
" 2	"	21	"	23
" 3	"	22	"	24
4	"	23	"	25
" 5	"	24	"	26
6	"	25	"	28, 29
7	EZRA	1	"	30
8	"	3	"	31
" 9	"	4	"	32
" 10	"	5	"	33
" 11	"	6	"	34
12	"	7	"	35
13	"	8 v. 21	"	36
" 14	"	9	"	37 to v. 22
15	NEH'MIAH 1		"	37 v. 22
16	"	2	"	38
17	"	4 to v. 13	"	39
18	"	4 v. 13	"	40
19	"	5	"	41
20	"	6	"	44
21	"	8	"	45
22	"	9	"	46
23	"	10	"	47
" 24	"	13	"	49
" 25	MATTHEW 2		"	42
" 26	PSALM 110, 111		"	50
27	ESTHER	1	"	51
28	"	2	"	52
29	"	3	"	53, 54
" 30	"	4	"	55
31	"	5	"	56

SECOND YEAR.

CALENDAR.		MORNING.	EVENING.
JANUARY	1	ESTHER 6	PSALM 57
"	2	" 7	" 58
"	3	" 8	" 59
	4	" 9 to v. 20	" 60, 61
	5	" 9 v. 20	" 62
	6	JOB 1	" 63
	7	" 2	" 64
"	8	" 3	" 65
	9	" 4	" 68 to v. 18
"	10	" 5	" 69 to v. 19
"	11	" 6	" 69 v. 19 & 70
"	12	" 7	" 70
"	13	" 8	" 71
"	14	" 9	" 72
"	15	" 10	" 73
"	16	" 11	" 74
"	17	" 12	" 75
"	18	" 13	" 76
"	19	" 14	" 77
"	20	" 15	" 78 to v. 24
"	21	" 16	" 79
"	22	" 17	" 80
"	23	" 18	" 81, 82
"	24	" 19	" 83
"	25	" 20	" 85
"	26	" 21	" 86
"	27	" 22	" 88
"	28	" 23	" 89 to v. 19
"	29	" 24, 25	" 89 v. 19
"	30	" 26	" 90
"	31	" 27	" 91
FEBRUARY	1	" 28	" 92, 93
"	2	" 29	" 94
"	3	" 30	" 95
	4	" 31	" 96
	5	" 32	" 97
	6	" 33	" 98
	7	" 34	" 99
	8	" 35	" 100
	9	" 36	" 101
"	10	" 37	" 102 to v. 15
"	11	" 38	" 102 v. 15
"	12	" 39	" 103
"	13	" 40	" 104 to v. 15
"	14	" 41	" 104 v. 15
"	15	" 42	" 105 to v. 22
"	16	PROVERBS 1 to v. 20	" 105 v. 22

· SECOND YEAR

CALENDAR.		MORNING.	EVENING.
FEBRU'RY	17	PROVERBS I v. 20	PSALM 106
"	18	" 2	" 107 to v. 31
"	19	" 3	" 107 v. 31 & 108
"	20	" 4	" 109
"	21	" 5	" 110, 111
"	22	" 6 to v. 20	" 112, 113
"	23	" 6 v. 20	" 114, 115
"	24	" 7	" 116, 117
"	25	" 8	" 118
"	26	" 9	" 119 to v. 24
"	27	" 10	" 119 to v. 48
"	28	" 11	" 119 to v. 72
MARCH	1	" 12	" 119 to v. 96
"	2	" 13	" 119 to v. 120
"	3	" 14 to v. 16	" 119 to v. 144
	4	" 14 v. 16	" 119 to v. 176
"	5	" 15 to v. 21	" 120, 121, 123
	6	" 15 v. 21	" 124, 125, 126
	7	" 16	" 128, 129, 130, 131
	8	" 17 to v. 15	" 132, 133, 134
"	9	" 17 v. 15	" 135
"	10	" 18	" 136
"	11	" 19	" 137, 138
"	12	" 20	" 139
"	13	" 21 to v. 17	" 140, 141
"	14	" 21 v. 17	" 142, 143
"	15	" 23 to v. 22	" 144
"	16	" 23 v. 22	" 145
"	17	" 24	" 146, 147 to v. 11
"	18	" 25	" 147 v. 11 & 148
"	19	" 26	" 149, 150
"	20	" 27	MATTHEW 1
"	21	" 28	" 2
"	22	" 29	" 3
"	23	" 31	" 4 to v. 17
"	24	ECCLES. 1	" 4 v. 17
"	25	" 2	" 5 to v. 21
"	26	" 3	" 6 to v. 16
"	27	" 4	" 6 v. 16
"	28	" 5	" 7
"	29	" 6	" 8 to v. 18
"	30	" 7	" 8 v. 18
"	31	" 8	" 9 to v. 18
APRIL	1	" 9	" 9 v. 18
"	2	" 10	" 10
"	3	" 11	" 11
	4	" 12	" 12 to v. 22

SECOND YEAR.

CALENDAR.	MORNING.	EVENING.
APRIL 5	JEREMIAH 1	MATTHEW 12 v 22
" 6	" 2 to v. 20	" 13 to v. 31
" 7	" 2 v. 20	" 13 v. 31
.. 8	" 3	" 14 to v. 22
9	" 4 to v. 19	" 14 v. 22
.. 10	" 4 v. 19	" 15 to v. 21
.. 11	" 5	" 15 v. 21
" 12	" 6	" 16
" 13	" 7 to v. 21	" 17
" 14	" 7 v. 21	" 18 to v. 21
" 15	" 8	" 19 to v. 16
" 16	" 9	" 19 v. 16
" 17	" 10	" 20 to v. 17
" 18	" 11	" 20 v. 17
" 19	" 12	" 21 to v. 23
" 20	" 13	" 21 v. 23
" 21	" 14	" 22 to v. 23
" 22	" 15	" 22 v 23
" 23	" 16	" 23 to v. 25
" 24	" 17	" 23 v. 25
" 25	" 18	" 24 to v. 29
" 26	" 19	" 24 v. 29
" 27	" 20	" 25 to v. 31
" 28	" 21	" 25 v. 31
" 29	" 22	" 26 to v. 36
" 30	" 23	" 26 v. 36
MAY 1	" 24	" 27
" 2	" 25	" 28
" 3	" 26	HEBREWS 1
4	" 27	" 2
5	" 28	" 3
6	" 29	" 4
.. 7	" 30	" 5
" 8	" 31	" 6
" 9	" 32	" 7
" 10	" 33	" 8
" 11	" 34	" 9
" 12	" 35	" 10
" 13	" 36	" 11
" 14	" 37	" 12
" 15	" 38	" 13
" 16	" 39	MARK 1
" 17	" 40	" 2
" 18	" 41	" 3
" 19	" 42	:: 4 to v. 26
" 20	" 43	.. 4 v 26
" 21	" 44	" 5 to v. 21

SECOND YEAR.

CALENDAR.		MORNING.		EVENING.	
MAY	22	JEREMIAH	45, 46	MARK	5 v. 21
"	23	"	47	"	6 to v. 30
"	24	"	48 to v. 25	"	6 v. 30
"	25	"	48 v. 25	..	7 to v. 24
"	26	"	49 to v. 23	"	7 v. 24
"	27	"	49 v. 23	"	8 to v. 27
"	28	"	50 to v. 21	"	8 v. 27
"	29	"	50 v. 21	"	9 to v. 30
"	30	"	51 to v. 35	"	9 v. 30
"	31	"	51 v. 35	"	10 to v. 32
JUNE	1	"	52	"	10 v. 32
"	2	LAMEN.	1	"	11
"	3	"	2	"	12 to v. 28
"	4	"	3 to v. 37	"	12 v. 28
"	5	"	3 v. 37	"	13
"	6	"	4	"	14 to v. 26
"	7	"	5	"	14 v. 26
"	8	EZEKIEL	1	"	15
"	9	"	2	"	16
"	10	"	3	ROMANS	1
"	11	"	6	"	2
"	12	"	7	"	3
"	13	"	13	"	4
"	14	"	14		5
"	15	"	18 to v. 19	"	6
"	16	"	18 v. 19	"	7
"	17	"	33 to v. 21	"	8
"	18	"	33 v. 21	"	9
"	19	"	34	"	10
"	20	DANIEL	1	"	11
"	21	"	2 to v. 24	"	12
"	22	"	2 v. 24	"	13
"	23	"	3	"	14
"	24	"	4	"	15
"	25	"	5	"	16
"	26	"	6	LUKE	1 to v. 39
"	27	"	7	"	1 v. 39
"	28	"	8	"	2 to v. 40
"	29	"	9	"	2 v. 40
"	30	"	10		3
JULY	1	"	11		4
"	2	"	12		5
"	3	HOSEA	1	"	6 to v. 20
"	4	"	2	"	6 v. 20
	5	"	3	"	7 to v. 36
	6	"	4	..	7 v. 36
"	7	"	5	::	8 to v. 26

SECOND YEAR.

CALENDAR.		MORNING.		EVENING.	
JULY	8	HOSEA	6	LUKE	8 v. 26
"	9	"	7	"	9 to v 37
"	10	"	8	"	9 v. 37
	11	"	9	"	10 to v. 25
"	12	"	10	"	10 v. 25
"	13	"	11	"	11 to v. 29
"	14	"	12	"	11 v. 29
	15	"	13	"	13
"	16	"	14	"	14
"	17	JOEL	1	"	15
"	18	"	2 to v. 15	"	16
"	19	"	2 v. 15	"	17 to v. 20
"	20	"	3	"	18 to v. 31
"	21	AMOS	1	"	18 v. 31
"	22	"	2	"	19 to v. 28
"	23	"	3	"	19 v. 28
"	24	"	4	"	20
"	25	"	5	"	21
"	26	"	6	"	22 to v. 31
"	27	"	7	"	22 v. 31
"	28	"	8	"	23
"	29	"	9	"	24
"	30	OBADIAH		I COR.	1
"	31	JONAH	1	"	2
AUGUST	1	"	2	"	3
"	2	"	3	"	4
"	3	"	4	"	5
	4	MICAH	1	"	6
	5	"	2	"	7
	6	"	3	"	8
	7	"	4	"	9
"	8	"	5	"	10
"	9	"	6	"	11
"	10	"	7	"	12
"	11	NAHUM	1	"	13
"	12	"	2	"	14
"	13	"	3	"	15
"	14	HABAKUK	1	"	16
"	15	"	2	JOHN	1 to v. 29
"	16	"	3	"	1 v. 29
"	17	ZEPH.	1	"	2
"	18	"	2		3 to v. 22
"	19	"	3	"	3 v. 22
"	20	HAGGAI	1		4
"	21	"	2	"	5
"	22	ZECHAR.	1	"	6 to v. 22
"	23	"	2	"	6 v. 22

SECOND YEAR.

CALENDAR.		MORNING.		EVENING.	
AUGUST	24	ZECHAR.	3	JOHN	7 to v. 32
"	25	"	4	"	7 v. 32
"	26	"	5	"	8 to v. 21
"	27	"	6	"	8 v. 21
	28	"	7	"	9
	29	"	8	"	10 to v. 22
"	30	"	9	"	10 v. 22
"	31	"	10	"	11 to v. 30
SEPTEMB'R	1	"	11	"	11 v. 30
"	2	"	12	"	12 to v. 20
"	3	"	13	"	12 v. 20
	4	"	14	"	13
	5	MALACHI	1	"	14
"	6	"	2	"	15
"	7	"	3	"	16
"	8	"	4	"	17
	9	ISAIAH	1	"	18
	10	"	2	"	19
"	11	"		"	20
"	12	"		"	21
"	13	"	4	2 COR.	1
"	14	"	6	"	2
	15	"	7	"	3
"	16	"	8		4
	17	"	9		5
"	18	"	10 to v. 20	"	6
"	19	"	10 v. 20	"	7
"	20	"	11	"	8
"	21	"	12	"	9
	22	"	13	"	10
	23	"	14	"	11
	24	"	15	"	12
"	25	"	16	"	13
	26	"	17	ACTS	1
	27	"	18	"	2
	28	"	19	"	3
"	29	"	20, 21		4 to v. 23
"	30	"	22		4 v. 23
OCTOBER	1	"	23	"	5 to v. 17
"	2	"	24 to v. 13	"	5 v. 17
"	3	"	24 v. 13	"	6
	4	"	25	"	7 to v. 30
	5	"	26	"	7 v. 30
	6	"	27		8 to v. 26
	7	"	28	"	8 v. 26
	8	"	29		9 to v. 23
	9	"	30		9 v. 23

SECOND YEAR.

CALENDAR.		MORNING.		EVENING.	
OCTOBER	10	ISAIAH	31	ACTS	10 to v. 34
"	11	"	32	"	10 v. 34
"	12	"	33	"	11 to v. 19
"	13	"	34	"	11 v. 19
	14	"	35	"	12
	15	"	36	"	13 to v. 14
	16	"	37	"	13 v. 14
	17	"	38	"	14 to v. 19
	18	"	39	"	14 v. 19
	19	"	40	"	15
	20	"	41	"	16 to v. 14
	21	"	42	"	16 v 14
	22	"	43	"	17 to v. 16
	23	"	44	"	17 v. 16
	24	"	45	"	18 to v. 18
	25	"	46	"	18 v. 18
	26	"	47	"	19 to v. 21
	27	"	48	"	19 v 21
	28	"	49	"	20 to v. 17
	29	"	50	"	20 v. 17
	30	"	51	"	21
	31	"	52	"	22
NOVEMB'R	1	"	53	"	23
"	2	"	54	"	24
"	3	"	55	"	25
	4	"	56	"	26
	5	"	57	"	27 to v. 21
	6	"	58	"	27 v. 21
	7	"	59	"	28 to v. 17
	8	"	60	"	28 v. 17
	9	"	61	GALAT'NS	1
	10	"	62	"	2
	11	"	63	"	3
	12	"	64		4
	13	"	65		5
	14	"	66	"	6
	15	I SAMUEL	1	EPHES.	1
	16	"	2	"	2
	17	"	3	"	3
	18	"	4		4
	19	"	5	"	5
	20	"	6	"	6
	21	"	7	PHIL.	1
	22	"	8	"	2
	23	"	9	"	3
	24	"	10	"	4
	25	"	11	COLOSS'NS	1

SECOND YEAR.

CALENDAR.	MORNING.		EVENING.	
NOVEMB'R 26	1 SAMUEL	12	COLOSS'NS	2
" 27	"	13	"	3
" 28	"	14 to v. 24	"	4
" 29	"	14 v. 24	JAMES	1
" 30	"	15	"	2
DECEMBER 1	"	16	"	3
" 2	"	17 to v. 30	"	4
" 3	"	17 v. 30	"	5
" 4	"	18	1 JOHN	1
" 5	"	19	"	2
" 6	"	20	"	3
" 7	"	31		4
" 8	2 SAMUEL	1	"	5
" 9	"	5	2, 3 JOHN	
" 10	JOSHUA	1	REVEL.	1
" 11	"	2	"	2
" 12	"	3	"	3
" 13	"	4	"	4, 5
" 14	"	5	"	6
" 15	"	6 to v. 12	"	7
" 16	"	6 v. 12	"	8
" 17	"	7 to v. 16	"	9
" 18	"	7 v. 16	"	10
" 19	"	8 to v. 14	"	11
20	"	8 v. 14	"	12
21	"	9	"	13
22	"	10 to v. 15	"	14
23	"	10 v. 15 to 28	"	15
24	"	22 to v. 21	"	16
25	Ps. 45 & ISA. 9 to v. 8		LUKE	2 to v. 38
26	JOSHUA	22 v. 21	REVEL.	17
" 27	"	23	"	18
28	"	24 to v. 19	"	19
29	"	24 v. 19	"	20
" 30	EXODUS	20	"	21
" 31	ECCLES.	12	"	22

PRACTICAL

SERMONS and ADDRESSES,

By Dr. A. H. Lochman, D. D.

These Sermons and Addresses were published at
the request of many of the friends and former par-
ishioners of the venerable author. Dr. Lochman
was pastor of Christ Lutheran Church for nearly
half a century. During these years he preached
many able and impressive sermons, some of which
made a deep impression on his hearers, and have
done much good.

As these sermons are highly instructive and
practical they will be useful to ministers as models
of sermonizing, and especially to laymen, on
account of the deep and fervent piety that per-
vades them all. They may also serve a useful purpose to be read at home on Sunday by those who
may be providentially prevented from attending
the public preaching of the gospel. They are also
well adapted to be read in church in lieu of a
preached sermon in the absence of the pastor.

In Dr. Lochman's Sermons we offer you a book
that is well worthy of your careful perusal. The
author was a highly respected father in our church,
having spent his life and labors for half a century
in her service; the sermons are eminently practical, pungent and spiritual, and will do good when
faithfully read.

The book contains an excellent portrait of the
venerable Dr. Lochman. Bound in cloth, octavo,
360 pages. Of 1900 copies printed, a few are left
over unsold. The original price was $1.50. But
we will now send it post free for 50 cents.

Address P. ANSTADT & SONS, York, Pa.

Luther's Smaller Catechism.

SECOND REVISED EDITION.

Explained, analyzed, illustrated with appropriate anecdotes, proverbs and examples, drawn from Scripture, history, biography, nature, and remarks of distinguished persons, by P. Anstadt, D. D., editor *Teachers' Journal, Christian's Guide*, author of *Bible Wine, Communion Addresses, Christian Catechism*, etc., etc. 308 pages octavo. Price post paid $1.25.

Rev. Treibly says, I have examined your *Illustrated Catechism*, and have come to the conclusion that it is a *most capital thing*. I hope you may dispose of a great many copies, for I think it will be a great help to preachers or any one else.

Dr. P. Born, Professor of Theology, Selinsgrove, Pa., kindly read some of the proof sheets and writes as follows :

"I am pleased with your method, especially in regard to the analysis of the several articles. It simplifies and aids in impressing and remembering the several points given under the respective heads. Your illustrations and anecdotes are pertinent and certainly add interest and value to the work. They give to abstract truths vividness and living forms. I hope the work will have an extensive circulation, for I think it is well calculated to do good."

A young minister in Pennsylvania writes, "I value the *Illustrated Catechism* a hundred times more than its price. The book looks interesting throughout, and I am eager to make a thorough examination of it, and then prepare a series of sermons based on the contents, with a free use of your illustrations. The volume ought to sell especially with young ministers."

Ministers or laymen who wish to have the work should send $1.25 and receive the book post free by return mail. P. ANSTADT & SONS, York, Pa.

Luther's Smaller Catechism.

PICTORIAL EDITION.

With Explanations and Proof Texts. Designed for Families and Sunday-schools. An introduction to the Illustrated Catechism. Illustrated with 20 beautiful, full page, half-tone Scriptural Pictures. By Rev. P. Anstadt, D. D., 132 pages octavo. Price, 25 cents, single copy, $2.40 per dozen.

This is the most elegantly gotten up edition of Luther's Smaller Catechism ever published in the English language. It is printed in large, clear type and fine book paper, and the fine pictures make it attractive to the eyes of the young. The explanations are plain and adapted to the understanding of the young and unlearned. There are also attached Family Prayers, Morning and Evening for a whole week, Children's Morning and Evening Prayers, Grace at the Table, and Morning and Evening Hymns.

It will be a very appropriate birthday or Christmas gift from parents to their children. Address

P. ANSTADT & SONS, YORK, PA.

Grace All=Sufficient.

A Sermon by Rev. E. Greenwald, D. D., Lancaster, Pa., on the text, "My grace is sufficient for thee." Ten pages, 10 cents.

Address P. ANSTADT & SONS, York, Pa.

THE SEVEN CALUMNIES.

A controversy between Rev. P. Anstadt, D. D., and Father Thos. McGovern, (Roman Catholic Bishop), on Transubstantiation, Purgatory, Salvation by Works, Infallibility of the Pope, Political Intrigues, Papal Bulls and Bible Burning. Second revised edition. Price 10 cents.

Address REV. P. ANSTADT & SONS, York, Pa.

A Christian Catechism,

designed for the use of

Families, Sunday Schools, Theological Students and Pastors.

By Rev. P. Anstadt, D. D.

152 Pages, with Pictorial Illustrations, Family Prayers for Morning and Evening, and appropriate Morning and Evening Hymns.

This Catechism is somewhat different in its construction from the usual form, being based on a regular course of Theology.

PRICES:

Bound in Boards . . . . 25 cts.
  " " Limp Cloth . . . . 30 cts.
Full Binding in Cloth . . . . 35 cts.

Send the amount for either of the above styles and the book will be sent by return mail.

Address,

P. ANSTADT & SONS,
YORK, PA.

WHAT THEY SAY OF THE CHRISTIAN CATECHISM.

I HAVE given the *Catechism* a careful examination. I am very much pleased with its evangelical quality and its simplicity. It is admirably adapted to the needs of the average catechumen

REV. J. W. RICHARD, D. D.,
Prof. Homiletics in Theological Seminary,

GETTYSBURG, PA.

THIS *Catechism* is distinguished from others by the fine quality of its paper, clear type, elegant binding, pictorial illustrations and logical arrangement. It will be found suggestive and useful. Write for sample copies.

REV. S. P. HALLMAN, A. M.,
in *Gospel Echoes*, Agusta, Ga.

THE BEST YET.—It has been our privilege to examine quite a number of catechisms, published by different houses and denominations, but if a young minister or an old one who has not had the advantages of a theological education, desires to obtain a catechism that will give him the cream of theological and Bible information, he need only get a copy of Dr. P. Anstadt's *Christian Catechism*, which is mainly designed for young people of advanced age and young students. It is the best of the kind we have ever seen. Send 25 cents in postage stamps to P. Anstadt & Sons, York, Pa., and you will receive a copy by return mail.

REV. G. W. CLINTON,
in Pittsburg Theological *Church Quarterly.*

Communion Wine.

—◆—

Or the unfermented juice of the grape the most appropriate kind of wine for the Lord's Supper. By Rev. P. Anstadt, D. D., York, Pa., pp. 79. Price 25 cents.

This is the title of a neatly printed book on a subject that has lately excited a deep interest among Christian temperance people. Many of them are at a loss to see how the duty of total abstinence. can be taught from the example of Christ on the basis of the so-called "one wine" theory, which insists that Christ made, and drank, intoxicating wine, and used it in the institution of the Holy Supper. The author has given an extended discussion of the subject of Bible Wines.

We append a few extracts from letters received. "I take his method of thanking you for this timely and very able production. If I had not previously entertained similar views, I do not see how I could help becoming a convert. I hope and believe it will have this effect upon others."

"I can not help expressing to you my gratitude and appreciation of your article on Communion Wine. It is the best and most conclusive I have ever read. I have for years abhorred the intoxicating cup commonly used on communion occasions, and yet could not see my way out of it."

"My first and strong impulse is to thank you with all my heart for a discussion so scholarly, so fair and temperate, and so conclusive, of a question so vital."

Every pastor, every Christian family, should have a copy. Sent free by mail for 25 cents.

Address P. Anstadt & Sons, York, Pa.

Short Communion Addresses.

By Rev. P. Anstadt, D. D., Editor of the Teach-ers' Journal, Scholar's Quarterly, Christian's Guide, Communion Wine. Justification by Faith, Christian Catechism, etc., etc. 100 pages with frontispiece, York, Pa. Price 25 cents.

———

They are composed of the most solemn and im-pressive matter, and may be of eminent service in suggesting valuable thoughts to ministers for such occasions. The matter supplies a vacancy in our literature.—*Prof. J. R. Dimm in Missionary In-stitute Journal.*

———

Communion Addresses is the title of a small volume of a hundred pages by Rev. P. Anstadt, D. D., containing several addresses delivered on communion seasons by the author. They are rich in thought, and will suggest to pastors many fitting words to be addressed to those who gather at the table of the Lord? We think it would be well for the members of our churches to ponder the words of this book before coming to the Lord's table? Published by the author at York, Pa, Price 25 cents.—*Messiah's Herald.*

———

A young minister writes: Communion Addresses received I am delighted with the little book ; it supplies me with the needed suggestions. I shall now begin to make short talks If I had seen an advertisement of such a book, I would have sent for it immediately.

Recognition in Heaven.

The Future Recognition of Friends in Heaven. By Professor Henry Ziegler, D. D., together with the Requisites to Recognition, by Rev. P. Anstadt, D. D., also extracts from the writings of Harbaugh, Schmucher, Stork, Luther, Melancthon, Knapp, Calvin, Tillotson, Doddridge, Baxter, Melville and others, together with extracts from the Poets. 200 pages, Anstadt & Sons, Publishers, York, Pa. Price 50 cents.

This is an elegantly gotten up book, neatly bound and printed in clear, large type, on fine book paper. An elegant half-tone engraving of the Ascension of Christ, serves as a fronticepiece, with the inscription: "I go to prepare a place for you. I will come again and receive you to myself; that where I am, ye may be also." John xiv. 2, 3.

The reading of this book will be a source of consolation to many bereaved souls, whose friends have indeed not been lost by passing through the valley of the shadow of death, but have only gone before, to welcome their loved ones to that happy home, where God shall wipe all tears from their eyes.

We advise all who wish to study the proofs from Scripture and reason, that we shall know each other in Heaven, and who wish to read the views of the most distinguished Christian writers on this subject, to procure a copy of this book. Send fifty cents in postage stamps or silver, and receive a copy free by mail ; or send a dollar note, check or bank, or P. O. M. Order for two or more copies, to give as a present to some of your bereaved friends.

Address

P. Anstadt & Sons, York, Pa.

A HELP TO
Family Worship.

Or Short Forms of Morning and Evening Prayers, for Five Weeks. With Prayers for Special occasions, Children's Morning and Evening Prayers, Grace at Table, and Morning and Evening Hymns, Compiled by Rev. P. Anstadt, D. D. P. Anstadt & Sons, Publishers, 300 pages octavo. Price $1.00.

These short forms are intended to be a help in conducting Family Worship. They are not designed to interfere with the free utterance of prayer by heads of families in their own words. But it is well known, that many pious Christians are not well qualified to lead in public worship. Some are diffident, or have not had the proper mental training, and have not command of appropriate words to edify in social prayer. It is to such mainly that this book is to be a help.

Let each person ask in silence beforehand for a collected frame of mind, and for the spirit of prayer, "Lord teach us to pray." Let this be the desire and prayer of each in kneeling before God. Nor let it ever be forgotten, that we have a great High Priest, through whom alone we have access to God, and that is the Spirit who helpeth our infirmities

In addition to the forms of prayers for morning and evening worship, the book also contains prayers for extraordinary occasions. Paraphrases of the Lord's Prayer, and Dissertations on Prayer by Matthew Henry and others. Send $1.00 and receive a copy of Help to Family Worship.

Address

P. Anstadt & Sons, York, Pa.

THE TEACHER'S CLASS BOOK

FOR SUNDAY-SCHOOLS.

This book is almost self-explanatory. To each quarter of the year there is a column for the names of teacher and scho'ars, followed by thirteen colum₁ s, one for the record of each Sunday of the quarter. In each column the attendances of every scholar may be marked with a cross (x), followed by the amount of his contribution and the number of Scripture verses recited by him. The total attendance, offering and number of verses learned each Sunday should be summed up at the foot of each column.

The quarterly report may be male by adding the figures from left to right for each scholar's at tendance, offerings and verses, and placing the results in the corresponding columns of the quarterly report. Transfer these figures to the quarterly columns in back of book and add the results in the same way for the annual repoit.

The offering for each Sunday should be placed in the envelope which forms the back cover of the book, and the total amount for each Sunday marked in the proper space on the envelope for the convenience of the Sunday school treasurer.

P. Anstadt & Sons, Publishers, York, Pa. Price 15 cents for single copy, $1.20 per dozen sent free by mail.

Ghrist the Model Preacher.

A Baccalaureate Address delivered before the Graduating Class of the Missionary Institute, Selinsgrove, Pa., June 24, 1880. By Rev. P. Anstadt. 12 pages. Price 10 cents. York Pa.

THE MODERN DANCE.

Discussed by two distinguished divines—"A time to dance."—Third edition. 16 pages, price 10 cents, or $1.00 a dozen.   P. Anstadt & Sons, Publishers, York, Pa.

This Discussion on Dancing has had a rapid sale.   The first and second editions are entirely exhausted.   As there are still calls for it, we now publish the third edition.   To this we add an essay by Rev. C. P. Pentecost, D. D.

Balls, or dances are frequently an annoyance to Christian parents and ministers.   A French danc-ing-master comes to town and opens a dancing-school.   Some of the "First Families" in town, occasionally also church members, send their child en to acquire this "graceful accomplish-ment," to "learn good manners," and "get into genteel society."   At the end of the quarter's teaching there is a grand ball to wind up with. Many church members would like to know "what harm there can be in this innocent amusement," and "why Christian people cannot be allowed to attend a respec able ball?"

These discussions, we think, will answer this question satisfactorily to every one who honestly desires to know what God's word teaches on this subject.

Send 10 cents and receive by return mail one copy, or $1.00 for 12 copies.

Address P. ANSTADT & SONS, YORK, PA.

The Bible Mode of Baptism.

This is the title of a closely printed, four page tract, containing the strongest arguments which can be produced that sprinkling is the Scripture Mode of Baptism.

For sale at the office of P. Anstadt & Sons Price: 100 copies, $3.00; 50 copies, $1.75; 25 copies, $1.00; single copy, 5 cents.

UNFERMENTED WINE
FOR SACRAMENTAL AND MEDICINAL PURPOSES.

Many inquiries have been made by ministers and church officers, as to where they can procure the best unfermented wine for communion purposes. There are wine growers in different parts of the country who make it a business to prepare this kind of wine.

The following items are taken from the circular of one of the oldest and most reliable establishments:

It is so very rich in the properties of the grape that it can be diluted about one-third, if desired.

It is so carefully prepared and so thoroughly clarified that there need be no fear of fermentation. Even after being opened it will keep for a long time in an ordinary cellar.

This Unfermented Wine is the pure juice of the grape.

This grape juice is from a very fine quality of Concord grapes, is carefully freed from all sediment and is kept entirely in vessels of porcelain and glass; it retains the delicate aroma, delicious flavor and life properties of the grape.

Why should Christian churches use the Wine of Commerce, most of which is adulterated with poisonous drugs, and often does not contain a drop of the fruit of the vine. We have been requested by one of the wine growers in Vineland, N. J., to act as agent for them in supplying churches with their Unfermented Wine. We are therefore prepared to supply it in any quantities desired. Samples can be seen at our office at any time. Wherever it has been used it has given perfect satisfaction, and the congregations that have used it once, never want to use any other kind.

PRICES:

12 Full Quarts,	$10.00	12 Full Pints, . . $5.00
1 Full Quart, . . . 1.00		1 Full Pint, . . 50

P. ANSTADT & SONS, York, Pa.

International Lesson System.

Its alleged Defects and Excellencies. By P.
Anstadt, D. D., Editor of Teachers' Journal,
Christian's Guide, Author of Christian Catechism,
Justification by Faith, Christ the Model Preacher,
etc., etc. Printed in pamphlet form. Published
by request of York County S. S. Convention.
Price 10 cents. P. Anstadt & Sons, York, Pa.

This add ess gives a brief history of the Primitive
Sunday-school, fifty years ago; the use of the
Question books in the Sunday-school, thirty years
ago, and then discusses the International Lesson
System. The alleged objections are stated and
answered.

Mr. William Reynolds, of Peoria, Ill., who has
traveled over every State of the Union in the interest of Sunday-schools, says, "This is the best address on the International Lesson Series that I
have ever heard." He took one hundred copies.
himself.

Send ten cents to P. Anstadt & Sons, York, Pa.,
and secure a copy by return mail, or twelve copies
for one dollar.

The Bible Catechism.

For young people, being an introduction to the
Christian Catechism. Prepared and edited by P.
Anstadt, D. D. Illustrated with Scriptural Pic-
tures. 32 pages, price 10 cents

It contains thirteen pictures, illustrative of some
of the most important events of Bible history in the
Old and New Testament, which will make it attractive and instructive to young people. It will
therefore be a very appropriate present from parents to their children.

Send 10 cents and receive a copy by return mail,.
or one dozen for $1.00.

Address P. ANSTADT & SONS, York, Pa.

Christian Endeavor Supplies.

We have been requested to act as agent for the Christian Endeavor supplies, including everything needed in conducting a C. E. Society, which will be sent on receipt of price, such as

Music Books, music and words, ...	35
Sample copies by mail, ...	40
Words only, in quantities, by express, .	12
" " by mail, ...	15
Secretary's Membership Record and Minute Book, revised, ...	1 50
Secretary's Roll Call Book, ...	35
Systematic Record Book of Committees, . .	50
(in lots of 5, 35 cents each.)	
Treasurer's Book, with supplement for monthly offering account, ...	
Handy Record Book, for Lookout and Prayermeeting Committees, in sets of 5, 8 cents each, ...	10
Record Lists, for Lookout and prayermeeting Committees, in lots of 5, 2 cents each, .	05
Active members' Chapel Wall Pledge, 36x54, printed on linen, ready to hang on wall,	1 75
Active Members' Chapel Wall Pledge, printed on heavy paper, 28x36, ready to hang on wall, ...	75
Topic Cards, for one year, per 100, ...	1 00
Daily Readings, for one year, per 100, . . .	1 50

C. E. CARDS.

Application Blanks, per 100, ...	50
Active Members' Pledge, per 100, ...	50
" " " gilt, bevel edge, per 100, ...	1 00

Associate Members' Pledge, gilt, bevel edge,
per 100, ... 1 00
Associate Members' Pledge, plain, per 100, . 50
Lookout Committee Cards, per 100, ... 75
Flower   "   "   gilt, bevel edge,
per 100, ... 75
Prayermeeting Committee Cards, per 100, . . 75
Invitation Cards, per 100, ... 75
Absentee   "   "   "   50
Monthly Offering Cards, per 100, ... 50
Suggestions for Lookout Committee, ⎫
    "   "   Prayermeeting "   ⎪ 3 cts. In
    "   "   Social   "   ⎬ lot of 5, 2
              "   Missionary   "   ⎪ cts. each.
    "   "   Sunday-school "   ⎭
Temperance Committee Pledge Cards, per 100,   50
    "   "   "   Book, with
room for 100 names, ... 03
Active Members' Pledge, 10x12, plain, . . .   10
    "   "   "   "   gilt, bevel
edge card, ...   25
Constitutions 02

SUNDAY SCHOOL TICKETS.

Blue and Red, with Scripture verses. We have
printed a large supply of these tickets. Price per
sheet of 154 tickets, 12 cents.

JUSTIFYING FAITH.

Its Nature and Effects. An Essay read at the
York County Sunday School Conference, held at
Jefferson, Pa., 1884. By Rev. P. Anstadt, D. D.
22 pages. Price 10 cents.

After the reading there was an interesting discussion, a hearty approval of the Essay by the
members of the Conference, and a request for its
publication.

Send 10 cents and receive a copy by mail.

P. Anstadt & Sons, York, Pa.

Popular Lesson Helps

—AND—

SUNDAY-SCHOOL

PERIODICALS.

THE TEACHERS' JOURNAL. Issued monthly, with 32 pages of copious explanatory notes on the International Lessons. Price 56 cts. a year.

LESSON QUARTERLY, for advanced scholars. Issued quarterly—32 pages, bound in cover. Price 12 cents a year.

INTERMEDIATE LEAF. A separate leaf for every Sunday. Price 8 cents per year.

PRIMARY LEAF. Is published monthly, 4 pages—price 6 cents a year.

OUR LITTLE FOLKS. A weekly lesson paper for the smaller children. 4 pages. Illustrated. Price 12 cents a year.

CHRISTIAN'S GUIDE. Issued monthly. This is an 8-page, illustrated paper, designed for young and old. Price for single copy 25 cents a year; for clubs of five or more to one address at the rate of 15 cents a year. Special attention is given to Christian Endeavor Societies. The paper contains one column of Explanatory Notes for every Sunday in the year. Samples sent free. Send all orders to

Rev. P. Anstadt & Sons,

YORK, PA.